Cooking to Die for...

Eric Moebius Morlin

Cooking to Die for.. is a Dreaming God Production. Copyright © 2016 Michael Christopher Markman All rights reserved. Nothing in whole or part may be reprinted without the author's written consent. All correspondence should be directed to: Dreaming God Productions, 25 Moore Ave, Merritt Island, Fl 32952
princeofautumn@yahoo.com

ISBN: 153764873X
ISBN-13: 9781537648736

DEDICATED TO:

God, Family, and Friends all of which have made the journey more tolerable, and without which… little has value… Cherish what you got, while you have it…

also dedicated to the memory of my father.
Who taught me to appreciate different kinds of foods, music, to read everything, and one of the better chefs. I've known… .

CONTENTS

	Acknowledgments	i
1	Catch those Falling Stars	3
2	Eavesdropping	8
3	Juan the Coroner man	12
4	Disclaimer	17
5	Punk Rock Kitchen	21
6	Hee Haw Hewn	26
7	Yokohama Mama	32
8	Dead Already Nostalgia	35
9	Sauchiehall Street	44
10	Saved by the Dead man	55
11	Just Beyond Sunset	56
12	Old Hewlitt's Sawmill	59
13	Rain through the Ceiling	65
14	Heart of Darkness	92
15	Day of the Dead	97
16	Deep in the Heart of Texas	101
17	The Island	105
18	Purple Bluish Christmas	111
19	Cross the Rubicon	98
20	EVAC	101

21	Raiders	127
22	Morte a Venezia	131
23	Rootftop Café	133
24	Always that One dirty Bastard	138
25	No one to name the Stroms	145
26	How to Maintain	147
27	DEAD, DEAD, DEAD	158
28	Drawn and Quartered	162
29	Alligator Soup	166
30	Intermission	168
31	Beyond Dreams	170
	Afterwards	178
	About the Author	180

ACKNOWLEDGMENTS:

As usually there are too many people that I need to thank… Folks who've helped my journey become more tolerable, and kept me going… Dorothy Markman, God, Jesus, Howard, Jimbo, Sarita, Johnny, Punk Ray, Rebekah Baker, Sheri Ferrel, Becky and Marv, Katherine Kube, Nicole and David, Ester Ames, David and Jennifer Fletch, Jennifer and Robert Wright, Mikel Weems, JJ Todd and David, Jennifer Raven, Willa, Katherine and Cary, Hanes, Mandy Roux, Erebus Erudite, Jimi James Dunn, John and Niccole, Danny, Dustin, Jaqueline, Deborah, HeatherHoney, Doron, Julian and Cynthia, Chris O' Shea, Warren Lapine, Jason Pradeep, Feeman, Barbara Johnston, Barbara, Holly and Adam Kitner, Erin Hoppes, David Orr, Robbie Coker, Dr. Samsam, Jason Norred, Zak Nash, Josh and Melinda, Yolli, Ernie, Jason Wray, Scott and Ann Baker, Floyd, Brian Moore, George Bosques, Sara Dunning, Greg Easthouse, Arron, Flynn, Janey, Lisa Sainz, Stephanie Williams, Billy Gunns, Dave Neuhohoho, Tammy, Shannon Marie, Ashley and Crawl, Stephanie Ralston, Vanessa Hyde, Brody, Julie Gunter, Lee Gray, Zak Broco, Laura Shepherd, Eric and Cherie, Larenda, Germ, Janey, Dan and Emily Richardson, Justus, Ron and Shirl, Tim and Kim, Em and Abby, John and Titiana, John and Robbie, Mike Quinn, Paul Cashman, Ripper, Niall Mad Elf, Fraser, M Holland, Hippie Chris, Trish Janey, Brent, Troy, James and Collette, Tracy, Sarah, Jordan, Marvin and Bailey, Jerry, Chris, Ian, Greg, Angie, David Seaton, Kate with an E, Damian, Isis, Maggot, Donnie, J'mal, Logan, Jennifer England, Samantha, Oscar Logger, Bam Bam, Alea, Bernard, Joe Armiger, Adam Baldwin, Eric Bloom, Kenny and Rose, Leo from Sparkle House, Lauren, Rachel, Jason, Wendy, Ted Keller, Shane Morton, Rob Thompson, Vii, Chevy and Devin, Kerry and Erich Ciotti, Shawn and Paulette, Alex Baez, AJ Hege, Kurt Kaff, Dennis Chandler, Ariel, Ariana, Kabuki, Robin and Rico, Wylde Bill, Chris Shu, Gigi and Lomar, Brian Palmer, Leslie Tony Hawk, Dennis Lovelace, Ronnie & Lisa, Andy Lytle, Kerry Mozingo, Trey Miller, Mario, Jack Bradley, Onionhead, Ben, Tiffany, Jason and Crystabell, Savannah and Amanda, Bryan Sullivan, John Alexander, Spider, Leon, Leroy Sly, Tyler, Tyler, Andrew Lochow, Shane Digby, Mark Stopper, Jinny Rucker, Goose Hands, Josh Childers, Steven Carter, Natasha, Mindy Chumita, Rya, Andrew, Jimmy, Eric Williams, Alex Loomis, Eric Tomlin, Ron the Van man, Courtney and Skylar, Jason and Jimmy, Architects of Fear, Mastadon, Wrath of a Dying Breed, Sister Sandoz, Bath salt Zombies, Zoembglas, Barefoot Ink, Transport Toys, Fiend without a Face, SS Hanami, My Dearest Friend, and many, many, many more…

Part I
<u>Dead Man's Kitchen</u>
Chapter 1
<u>Catch Those Fallen Stars While they're Weeping</u>

"The years before the plague of the Eaters, was to watch other plagues sprout up like orchids.... " – Milla Pershgome

Zaire
1976

The first outbreak of the Ebola virus. There is an 88% mortality rate; with 280 of the 318 people who contracted the disease dying.

Fort Detrick
Frederick, Maryland, U.S.
1977

The United States moves to weaponize the disease after confirming with agents in the Middle East that the Soviet Union is working on a similar project…

Democratic Republic of Congo
1995

315 contract the disease, only 250 die. The vector for the disease is thought to be apes that are being used for "Bush meat." This is to say, that hunters who killed apes would accidentally cut their hand during the food preparation process and then later contract the disease. It is highly virulent with an incubation period of anywhere between 2 and 21 days.

Uganda
2000
An outbreak of Ebola kills 224 out of 425. The majority of those who died were caregivers for others sick with the disease, including doctors. As well as persons who had attended funerals for the diseased, and made contact with the body.

Republic of Congo
2001
43 out of 57 die in the latest outbreak of Ebola.

Guangong Province China
2002
The first case of atypical pneumonia, later given the moniker of Sudden Acute Respiratory syndrome (SARS)

China, Vietnam, Hong Kong
2003
The World Health Organization (WHO) issues a global alert for a severe form of pneumonia of unknown origin to all persons in these regions.

by the end of the year 800 are dead. The suspected vector is a mammal known as the Civet.

Dead Man's Kitchen

China
2005

A flood in South China kills 50,000. It is later uncovered that a new strain of the already highly contagious SARS virus surfaces. It is suspected that the Chinese were working on their own biological weapons project and something went wrong. The disease was not only highly contagious, but cause a feral almost animal like ferocity in patients.

Other stories would surface within the intelligence community, about those who died coming back to life and pursuing all other living persons with extreme prejudice. There were no survivors on record. Media coverage: non-existent.

UGANDA AND DEMOCRATIC REPUBLIC OF CONGO
2007

The outbreak in Congo kills 187 out of 264.
West Uganda is less severe with only 37 dying out of 144.

DEMOCRATIC REPUBLIC OF CONGO
2008

An adapted strain of the Ebola virus surfaces in primates, causing them to become highly aggressive, with assistance from the United States Military the governments initiate a scorched earth policy. The entire populations fo of ████████ and ████████ are killed. The story gets no media coverage.

AUSTRALIA
2010

An unusual outbreak is said to have been quashed by the

Australian military, when a contagion broke out in the ▓▓▓ township. The media story describes it as a toxic chemical explosion... all 2,083 members of the community are considered to be fatalities.

SAUDI ARABIA
APRIL 2012
The Middle East respiratory syndrome (MERS) makes its first betacoronavirus is first identified and said to be the biological agent involved in of. 100 die.

TUNISIA
2013
The 8th outbreak in as many months, since the first appearance of the MERS Coronavirus (MERS-CoV), but this strain appears to have mutated like previous strains of SARS, and EBOLA. The nation's healthcare services appears to be unable to impede the spread of the contagion, and the governmental infrastructure appears on the verge of collapse.

Chapter 2
Eavesdropping

December 31, 2012

There is a room with people talking, as people do. You are sitting at a table drinking a Shiraz, when you over hear them.

****

"Someone already has a vaccine for it…"
"how do you know?"
"Well, they had a lab tech who pricked their finger, and there was never a follow up story about them dying."
"So what."
"Well, the media would follow that, cause the shits Ebola and you can bet Germans were glued to their new… No story of a false alarm. No need to worry anymore. Instead nothing. Sure it could have been a snafu, they're fine didn't contract it. Only, no feel good story with kittens. They could have covered up a death, but knowing the krauts it would have been discovered."
"Which leaves, they've found a cure and didn't tell anyone,"
"Indirectly, because if they didn't develop a vaccine, but their employee got the disease and they didn't die… They would then have someone whose body had produced antibodies for that strain which could be used to create a

vaccine."

"Huh. So, How'd you find out?"

"some guy posted the info out Twitter, while he was watching the plague numbers for Ebola, and no one helping... started to post on the WHO page and a couple others asking about this person in Germany, and pointing out hey, this company must have a vaccine."

"Which shamed, don't ask me how, seems to have shamed the Europeans into admitting they have a vaccine, enough to wipe out this outbreak."

"Okay, but that doesn't explain why you know about it, really."

"Oh, I got a call from some of the Meat Heads over at Fort Detrick, down in..."

"I F'ing know where Ft. Detrick is Will. I told you I worked with George W. Merck."

"Oh, F*ck I thought you knew him from the Pharmaceutical side of,"

"Nope, that's also how I met Ira L. Baldwin, back at Camp Detrick..."

"and Nakki..."

"Nakkamoro, he was affiliated with the Camp 731 thing with the Nipponese. How can you not know this?"

"Look, that isn't why I'm here, or not directly. The event is going to happen. The NSA know about it because they've been watching the kid since he was in diapers."

"Say what, so why hasn't someone done something..."

The other man laughs.

"Oh, don't tell me what I think you're about to tell me."

"Project Theseus. We think we found it."
"It has something to do with the twitter post."
"They've been watching the guy since he was a baby. You said that,
and no one whacked the kid, First, because it was a kid, and then,"
he pauses to let the other man finish his sentence,
"and later because of orders from higher on up."
"How high?"
"Skies the limit I'm afraid, when they tried to by-pass the order we had agents in countries all over the world get snatched the same night, and then he triggers the Iraq debacle,"
"no, who the Hell has that kind of clearance ," the man pauses.
"We sold them the WMDs, Perhaps it's his sense of karma."
"wait. You said event is going to happen? Call it off. Now, do not proceed."
"It's already done man, there's not a thing we can do."
The other man laughs, and says, "now I understand why we're having the fancy aged Rum, and cigars."
"Only live once."
"True indeed."

Just then someone comes up to give you a card. It has the following recipe on it.
****

Mayonaise:
2 egg yolks
¼ cup heavy cream
1 clove garlic
2 ½ teaspoons fresh lemon juice
2 teaspoons white wine vinegar
½ teaspoon guldens mustard
1 teaspoon salt
1 ½ cup virgin olive oil

Mix together and chill.

Chapter 3
Juan the Coroner Man

Cocoa Beach, Fl
November 15, 2013

Juan Rinetoot pulled into the Waffle House. Normally, he wouldn't go there. He was more a Denny's guy. Only when the guy on the stretcher, in the back of his van, sat up. All bets were off. Juan drove a van for the county coroner's office, and he'd had bodies make awful noises, and produce worse sounds, but what this body was doing went outside the bounds of what he felt... appropriate.

So, Juan went into the Waffle House to wait for his nerves to settle. He hoped that guy in the back would just lay down and shut up. This also became somewhat humorous. What if the paramedics had been wrong? Only it wasn't just that he'd done a follow up for the coroner's office checking heartbeat, before zipping 'em up to take back to county. Juan had seen the state the body had been prior to the zipping up, the guy had a hole straight through his intestines. There was no way that guy was alive, only Juan could see the body on the stretcher in the back of his truck writhing around like a big black worm.

Again and again ambulances drove by along A1A, and

Juan could feel his phone vibrating in his pocket.

    A couple came in just then, to sit at a booth not far from Juan. They complained about a guy in the back of the parking lot acting aggressive toward them. After they told the waitress, she'd told the cook, who went outside. He came back inside, bleeding from the inside of his forearm. Juan knew this went along with all the other craziness that was in his head. The waitress Sally Ann called the Sheriff's Department. Juan was drawn to watch as the two Deputy Sheriffs spoke with the man outside. They then closed on him to cuff him, when he bit one of the officers in the face. The man had latched onto the officer's lower lip and just held on. All the while the officer is howling," Get him off me," Which sounds far less coherent when someone is tearing your lip off.

    The officer keeps screaming.

    The second officer is hitting the biter now, and trying to shove a metal baton into the other man's mouth. Finally, the man who bit the officer's mouth opens and the officer is able to pull free. A long strip of ragged meat dangles free from the officer's face. The other officer fires at the biter. The bullets hit him in the center of the chest, but he is running at the full bore. The officer barely gets off a swing with is baton, and the man falls. "Stay down," The officer says laughing, "fucking monstrous piece of garbage," not even trying to close the distance between them.

Inside the waitress is wrapping the cook's arm. The waitress calls the manager to tell him that the cook is going to have to go home, and that either they have to get another cook in, or she is going home.
"No, I will not cook, and wait tables," the waitress says, "either you get your ass in here and cook, or you can find a new cook and a new waitress." When the officer's fire their weapon the waitress almost jumps out of her seat. "You hear that," Sally asks," Yeah, that was the cops shooting that guy. I don't get paid for this kind of bullshit. I'm going home." There is a pause, and then she laughs and says, "Fire me, and then no one will work for you. Charlie got bit by that guy, and he's leaving too.. You gonna fire him too? There's people shooting at your people here you jerk."

Sally continues talking, as across the room Juan signals to her he is getting a refill from behind the counter. She gives him the thumbs up. He also grabs extra cream. Juan then looks back to see that big black, zippered worm flopping about in his truck. Juan leaves Sally a $20 on the counter, so she can see it as he is leaving.

That is when Juan and Sally hear a second shot, then a third. The officers come in through the front door. One officer is bleeding from his face, He is holding a t-shirt against the wound, and blood still occasionally drools down from the drenched cloth. Juan decides there are too many people with bite marks in the restaurant, and he'd rather take chances out in the van, at least there the body is in the bag.

Only Juan knows he can't stay here. The officers are preoccupied as Juan slips out the front door heading for his van. He doesn't notice there are more of those things across the street attacking a tourist. Instead he drives toward work to return the van.

This might be his last night on the job.

Juan had been experimenting with making his own cheese, and so thinks about how if things don't work out, at least he can eat some good cheese when he gets home.

This is his recipe:

****

Two Cheeses:
You will need:
A large cook pot
1 galloon milk
1 tsp sea salt
cheese cloth
colander/ strainer
¼ cup apple cider vinegar
3 teaspoons lemon juice

Directions:

Fill large cooking pot with milk and heat on med high, until it just starts to boil. Don't boil it if you can avoid it. It doesn't taste as good. Check temperature throughout, and make sure to stir so the milk does not burn or stick to the sides. When the milk has reached approximately 195 F; remove from oven, and add vinegar, and salt. Stir into mixture.

Let stand for ten minutes.

Set colander in the sink with a bowl underneath, put cheese cloth in colander so that it will allow you to collect all the solid curds, what should drain out is a yellow soupy liquid. Let your cheese drain in your cheese cloth for several hours. The yellow goop that is leftover is called whey.
By itself Whey is a good source of protein.
However, this recipe requires you put your whey on the stove again. Same temperature, and everything. Once you see it start to clot up, remove it from the heat, like you did last time, and add in your lemon juice. Salt to taste. Let it cool, and then drain in another colander with a cheese cloth in it. This gives you a **Ricotta Cheese**.

CHAPTER 4
DISCLAIMER:

I know, I know... normally, you'd find this toward the front, but I don't do things in the traditional fashion. I can only point out that this is exactly the kind of thing a disclaimer like that couldn't have warned you about. Only I also do share certain traditional values, and the traditional baggage that goes with that. So...

If you're this, and expect me to be that, or even this... I might be and do something totally different from this and that, leaving you on a totally different footing than you started. Oh, and if you're a stickler for grammar and start freaking out about switching from past and present tenses, I could say that this is because this story isn't just set in the past, present, or future; but all three mutually.

(if you keep reading I might offend you).

I also cuss. I also censor myself. At times I will find cussing is totally inappropriate. I admit that happens less. There are adult situations in this book. There is acts of coitus interuptus, although, not actually outside the marriage bed. If I don't offend you, awesome. You are cooler than everyone else. Especially my detractors, they all blo... blog... they all blog donkey clicks. Looking for internet traffic in all the wrong places they are.

Oh, and bad sh*t happens to people. I mean, I paint ugly pictures, and I might even make 'em sound pretty.
I'm bad about that. I also paint an idealized world with idealized heroes, but not idealized ideologies. I believe in God. Judge me a hypocrite if you dare, but... I think I'm

Eric "Moebius" Morlin

fucking allowed to be conflicted. Irony, since I offend Christians and non-Christians alike. Go me.
So, if you would get offended by cussing, but read about rape or murder. I'll tell you, you should see both are bad, or something else is conflicted in you. Who hurt you before? Because I ain't them. Neither are you, but you're who you hurt if you walk the path of the hungry. Who are they now? If you understand the shame, anger, shame guilt cycle. You know, pain from people you love… who didn't intend to hurt you, but… whom hurt you none the less. Vice Versa. Of course, I'm also saying if you really love them, look at that word Vice Versa real careful, and process it.

The reason they are still stuck is that whole… forgiveness bit.

You want to chat about that sometime awesome. However, my book is about ideologies and striving for madness or unattainable perfection… Wish me luck.

Eric "Moebius" Morlin

Chapter 5
Punk Rock Kitchen
Naw'lins, LA
Nov 15, 2013

Liam had found the abandoned warehouse and thought for the first time, how being a chaos magnet might pay off… There was at least a dozen kilns, and a foundry in the place. It was the score of a life time. Liam almost cussed when he saw the cnc routers. The machines were still in good shape…
Liam found himself looking around the room to make sure he wasn't on camera. That's when he heard it… It sounded like a cat in heat at first, then… something not nice. Mike got out his knife and looked for a piece of rebar. Finally he discovers a huge wrench like you'd use on a tractor trailer. It is almost a solid piece of metal
    When it finally comes out of the dark at him, he sees it's a woman. Only, she doesn't look human aside from the clothes she is wearing, and make like a wild animal. She is running full out. Before he can do anything else, he just swings and hits her right between the eyes with the wrench. He can feel her skull cave in beneath the force of his blow.
She falls back like a large tree, hits the ground, and her head bounces off the concrete. Liam can't stop himself for swinging a few more time.
"I knew it was too f'ing good to be true," he says.

He leaves the way he came. In a half hour he's out in front Jackson Cathedral. Tarot readers and artists sit around the square as usually, and a jazz band plays for money in front of the church itself.

Liam can't stop thinking about the warehouse. That thing, that woman, whatever she was. He tells himself what he saw can't be real, but if it isn't he has just murdered someone.

Suddenly a woman screams, a man in the crowd just leaned over and took a chunk out of the top of her shoulder. It is a bloody mess. He suddenly wishes he hadn't left the wrench behind, and then he sees the man's eyes. One of them is whitish blue, the other looks like someone gouged it out. There are other gouges as well, in the man's face and neck, like someone had tried to fight him off.

Finally someone shanks the guy, A knife in one ear. The man falls, and the woman he bit is laying there in someone's lap, as they hold a cloth pressed up against it, to staunch the blood flow. Liam can't help but stand there.

People talk to the woman softly, but they are helpless. Finally, she lets out a shuddering breath and stops breaking. The man who was holding her, is saying, "Please don't go baby, wait for the ambulance with me," but she doesn't seem to hear.

They all sit or stand around in silence, except for the weeping man. When suddenly, a miracle. She sits up. Liam can tell though, as soon as she sees her face that; nobody is home. Liam yells to the man, "get away from her," and the man looks puzzled, "What?" and then she's turned from where she sat between his legs. She practically mounts him, and starts to eat his face.

At this point, all Hell breaks loose, people start moving away from the carnage, as they look for somewhere safe. Liam is already making his way toward a squat one of his friend Ted operates a soup kitchen out of... It looks like a lot of the other folks got the same idea, only as soon as

Dead Man's Kitchen

they arrive, Liam sees that Jenny Fox has a bite mark on her. He goes to talk to Ben in private. The place used to be an old factory of some kind, and has a two way mirror that looks down on the floor of the building. Ben has built a house within the building. Liam navigates his way to Ben's room, and upon finding him tells him, all that he's seen.

"Yeah, I've been hearing crazy stuff like that all day," Ben says, and the folks who've gone done to Charity Hospital haven't been coming back."

"You've noticed Jenny's been bit right," Liam asks, and Ben looks down to see her sitting there, pulling the sleeve of her jacket down over the bite mark, as if to cover it. Liam suspects she already knows what is going to happen to her. We need to get rid of her, she's going to become one of those things. Ben nods, and goes down to talk to Jenny.

"Hey Jenny," he says.

"Hey Ben," she smiles. It doesn't even look forced. They've known each other a long time. Those who are in the know, know that Ben has had a thing for Jenny for a long time.

"Why didn't you tell me you got bit? You know you're taking a chance with the lives of everybody here." She immediately starts balling her eyes out. Liam feels bad, but doesn't want to die either. Ben and Jenny walk to the back of the squat to talk, and after awhile there is a solitary, "bang", then silence.

Liam doesn't see Ben for a long time after that, and for a little while he is worried, and then Ben comes downstairs to say he's making specialty tonight.

"Flaming Roadkill."; this is his recipe.

****

Flaming Roadkill

What you'll need:
½ pound of meat, bacon, road kill
(*use what you got, des ne?)
1 large chopped onion
1 cut long grain rice
water for the rice
1 Tablespoon malt vinegar
1 teaspoon brown sugar
½ cup cream or evaporated milk
1 Tablespoon Tabasco

Spices (if available):
1 teaspoon dill
2 teaspoons paprika
1 teaspoon dried garlic
if not use a boullion cube, and no salt.

Directions:
1) cook meat and onions together until done, and the meat's fat is rendered.
2) in same pot add uncooked rice, spices, brown sugar, vinegar, tabasco, water.
You might wonder why cook rice with the beef. The answer is so that it will suck up all the fats and liquids from the ingredients.
3) 5 minutes before rice is done, add cream, then finish cooking.
4) enjoy with all your senses. Live another day.

Chapter 6
Hee Haw Hewn

it ain't the redneck who poisoned
the air, instead he still grows your food,
perhaps he talks slower,
than you think he should…
it ain't the Mexican who stole
your job, and sent it far away,
and yeah, we all buy into these
dumb sterotypes,
just in a much subtler way…
us vs. them,
me vs. you,
this his posse, that your crew,
and nothings wrong with what you do…
I mean, we all want to protect the
folks we love… sadly,
even when they ain't true…
Instead of pushing them to become
something else, we push them,
so they can push us back …

Hurricane, Mississippi
Nov. 14, 2013

Henry had been working on the farm all afternoon. However, around 4p.m. the weather started to pick up, and he knew they were in for a storm. It was almost 4:30 before he had all the animals fed, and put up…
and by then the storm had worked itself into a full on frenzy. The power was still working, but the phone was out. Henry only had a landline. Cell phones didn't work out here at all.
Only when Henry saw Billy Asher pulled up to the front

gate, he knew there was real trouble.

Billy Asher was married to Henry's cousin Tammy, and she was right there with him pulling up latch on the gate. As Billy drove in, Tammy closed the gate after him… They drove up the hill to the house, and got out. Bill could see no sign of the young 'uns, and Tammy was wailing something fierce…

"Y'all okay?" Henry asked from his front porch. He was already standing, and on his way down the steps, but Billy yelled out, "Stay back Henry… Me and Tammy might be sick already…"

Henry looks at them, they both look fine, except Tammy seems to be bleeding. Henry starts to reach for her, "Good lord, what happened to you…"

Only Billy stands between them, and says, "I'm telling you stand back, Henry… Haven't you been watching the news!?!? Look the kids are in back…" Tammy says, "Just follow Billy," and points for Henry to follow Billy. He opens the hatchback on their vehicle. Henry can see the front of the car is separated by a sheet of visqueen that was stapled to the ceiling of the car.

The kids are there, but he makes no move to help them out…

At first Henry thinks they might have killed 'em, but he can see the kids trying to reach out to their father. Henry hears Billy talking, "Y'all stay back, now… I told you, poppas sick… We need to go to the hospital before… "

Maggie, age seven is already reaching out for her father, and he is saying, "I want to hug you too, baby. Only we can't take any chances…"

"What the Hell is going on…"Henry says, as he goes to stand between the children and their father, thinking he might have finally gone and lost it…

Billy says," Just turn on the news… Things are real

bad… We're gonna try to meet up with Doc Turner, but… He said if we contracted this thing… He doesn't know what to do with it, other than keep us hydrated and hope we're one of the lucky ones…"

"Lucky ones…? what the," Only Tammy and Billy are already climbing into the front seat of the car. Henry helps the children out, and then sends 'em up to the house… Henry starts to reach for Tammy through the window, but Billy screams out, "Dear God, don't Henry… You may be the only way for the children to survive this mess…"

"You sure y'all haven't gotten tangled up in drugs or something," Henry asks.

Billy responds with a laugh, and says, "Yeah, Henry… You finally caught on about our secret Meth Lab…"

"Tell the children we love them," Tammy says, "and I want you to hug them for me… and…" she starts weeping. "I," Henry starts to say, but Billy is already in reverse, driving back out to the gate. Tammy stays in the car when they pull up the the gate. Henry can only imagine she has lost it… Whatever is going on, must be bad… Billy opens the gate, drives out, and closes the gate… without even taking a glance back.

Henry and the children are left alone with the storm.

Henry has been making mead down in the basement. There are at least a dozen shelves of bottled mead, and another dozen or so of Muscadine. Calhoun and Pontotoc counties are both Dry Counties, but Henry only makes for personal consumption, and supports only moderate use. There are also dozens of shelves with the larger (5 Gallon) gas bottles filled with water, and then several more shelves with bottles of mead with fermentation locks in them.

This is Henry's recipe…
****

Henry's Mead

You'll need:

5 gallon gas water bottle
(**don't use the blue plastic bottles**: Clear glass only, as plastic ones to break down when heated by the fermentation process, and that plastic becomes a poison).
Fermentation lock
funnel
big metal pot
2 gallon Spring water
1 gallon honey
thermometer
1 package yeast (see notes…)

optional: (not saying do this all at once, just saying these are all things you could try, experiment… develop your own taste unique to your tastes…)
blueberries, apple, pear, peach slices, watermelon, elderberries, strawberries, kewies, never tried bananas… If I used black berries I'd probably just squeeze 'em, and add the juice (seeds), grapes, coconut, carrot (would probably juice), beets (if you're into it…. Sometimes a hint of a flavor makes things interesting), cherries, apricots, plum, cranberries..

Directions (how to get there):

First you must prepare your must… If you were making a grape wine this would be the crushed fruit juice with all your particulate matter, this takes up about 20% of your young wine mix.

The word Must comes from Latin Vinum Mustum, which means, "young wine". In honey wine the must is made by heating the and slowly adding honey, and stirring it in until it is fully dissolved.

Note: if you are sure about the safety of your water source, then you'll want to boil your water, and let it cool down. Let it cool so it is warm/hot, then add all the honey and stir it 'til it dissolves. The reason you don't want to have it too hot is actually, the yeast… (You don't want the Must too hot, as this can kill your yeast).

You'll want to put any optional fruit in your bottle, and used your funnel to add your Must… add some cool water. Check your water temperature… The water should be below 90 F. Add a packet of yeast, and put in the fermentation lock… You can also let the mix

Now put the mixture in a cool dark place. The mix will bubble a bit from the yeast you added, which is why you have that fermentation lock… You'll need to let the mix sit for 5 to 6 weeks, if it is still super fizzy after the end of that time you'll want to wait another week or so before bottling…

After you bottle it, let the beer sit for a while. You wouldn't want to drink green beer, figure… you probably wouldn't want green mead either… so, figure let it set for a couple of month s to a year. The longer it sits, the better it will taste, and also the higher the percentage of alcohol.

Dead Man's Kitchen

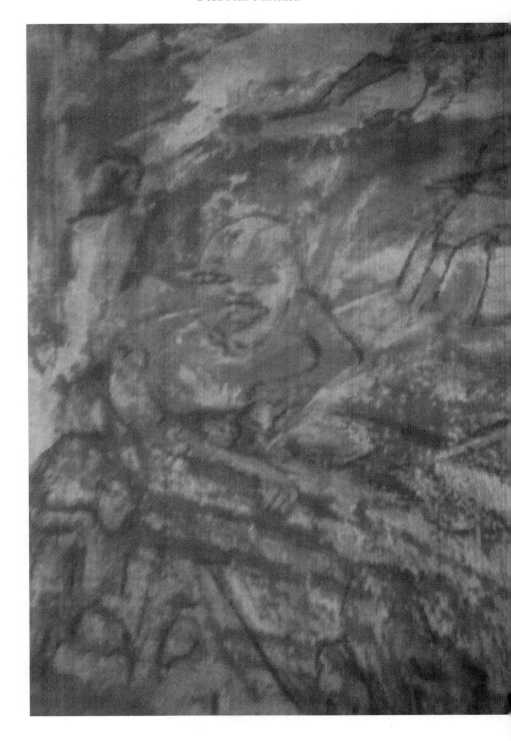

Chapter 7
Yokahama Mamma
Yokohama, Japan
Nov. 15, 2013

One of the first Japanese cities to open their port to foreign trade, and one of the first to fall. No one ever finds out what the vector was for the biological agent that eviscerated the city, but they know it started in the subways.
A sick woman boards the train. The train is packed as usual, pushers, help to make sure everyone can get on board. No one notices the ill woman, or this isn't entirely untrue. For some reason, as noble as the Japanese culture is, the creepers hang in the subways looking for the occasional stray not wise enough to get on the women only trains. The woman passed out under the crush of bodies, but her body was still warm with fever as she is pressed against the man behind her, holds her up.
In the press of bodies no one notices she dies not short after, most of them on the way to work. The slimy occupants think they've scored until the first man screams. The man holding her up, had put his fingers in her mouth, and she snapped her jaws shut. The taste of blood sends the eater into a frenzy, as she clamps onto the jugular of the man next to her. Blood gushes from the wound in the man's neck, painting those around him. The blood gets in people's eyes. It makes the floor slick, and several people fall and get trampled. The dying man is held up by those closest to him. The woman gets another man's ear, another man's cheek. She bites, and tears into anything she can reach. The man behind her tries to lock her into a choke hold. He is not very skillful, but he starts to try to

choke her when she sinks her teeth deep into the muscle of his forearm. He screams it is a howl. People try to vacate that part of the train car, but it is too crowded. No one notices the second eater starting to awaken in their midst, and another. It was like locking a rabid dog in tiny room full of people. Those who've turned climb over the bodies, or slither about on the floor. One man falls as an eater bites into his calf muscle. In a matter of minutes the train is a blood bath, by the time it pulls into the station, more people have turned…

When the trains doors open, they go to greet the pushes, and those who were waiting with open arms and hungry mouths, in a matter of hours the city is starting to be overrun.

Eric "Moebius" Morlin

CHAPTER 8
Dead Already Nostalgia

I told here,
we've got 'til forever,
didn't know she was already dead...
I mean, aren't you a singularity,
of everything you've ever said?
or is your movie not yet over,
because if it was it would be doing flips...
fap, fap, fap, fap, fap...

Cocoa, Fl
Nov. 15, 2013

Erin had just found out she was sick, and then the world had gotten sick...
Right after Mike had proposed, and she'd said, "Yes."
planned a crazy beautiful wedding, and...

Life could be a dirty b*tch sometimes...
and this felt like one of them.

Erin had found out she had cancer, and she couldn't help but keep thinking how it could kill Mike. She laughed to herself... She knew on one level she was being selfish, protecting herself from having to see Mike hurt... He would see it as betrayal... Guys are like children, but she totally understood, and...
She'd spoiled him. She'd been doing all the accounting. IF she didn't make him, he wouldn't even balance his check book.

Mike, for all his airs of being, "ready to take on the world 24 hours a day, 7 days a week..." would be the first one to admit Erin, lent him... balance. She kept him in check with himself, that swaggering, self-sabotaging, son of a... Which made all this the more crazy. She was tough, how the heck did she have cancer... As if, being tough, or standing up for what you believe in... Could create a force field against sickness and death...

The stuff she read on, Chinese medicine, associates different sickness with emotional states. Yeah, she felt more like Moses, than Christ when she thought about healing... Hit it with a stick, and say," Water come forth," instead of, "you are forgiven." Either way she still had cancer, and as much as she loved Mike in that same crazy closet co-dependent kinda way, and... She knew he wasn't ready for her to die...
and it was Nov. 15, and... she had to go to see Dr. Reich and... at 5:30 p.m.
She wasn't ready...

****
So, She started to make lunch. It was ham and egg noodles. Mike's favorite.
Now's as good as any to share a recipe:

Ham and Eggnoodles

You'll need:

A canned ham, unless you got a pig handy.
Bag of egg noodles.
4 fresh eggs
¼ cup milk
1 teaspoon salt
Parmesan Cheese
A big pot
a big pan
a bowl
colander/strainer

Directions:

Add a teaspoon of iodized salt to the water in the pot. Heat it so the water boils, add your egg noodles.

In the pan cut up your ham, and let it cook slowly… might even cover it for a while, let it caramelize… (Caramelization is the browing of sugar, which results in a caramely brown color, as it slowly starts to carbonize the meat… too long it burns…)

In your bowl add eggs, and milk, and whisk the eggs with the fork… (a whisk is a way of whipping your eggs, or stirring them using a fork in a light quick movement…) It should all look uniform in color when done…

Taste your egg noodles and when they're ready dump them into the colander… Once you've got out most of the water, pour the noodles onto the ham, then pour the egg onto the noodles… stir it together until all the egg is cooked, then serve with parmesan cheese…

****

After lunch is over… They sit in that afterglow, almost post coital cuddly in nature. They kiss for a while, and she holds Mike never wanting to let go her and Mike looks more peaceful than she's seen him in ages. The making out leads to hungry intimacies, they move around the house with a slow subtle feverishness. The house is probably fogging up from the outside, as they bite and kiss on each other… They linger on every touch, as if it is their last…

The language of their hands is that of rock climbers exploring an abandoned paradise, lost to the rest of the world, in those long drawn out kisses. Mike drags his teeth along her neck gently, pulling on the surface skin, then slowly releasing in feline aggression…

Mike takes his time carrying Erin toward the bed room, occasionally they end up on the edge of a table, or … Mike massages her feet as he pushes into her, and both of them explore the others with their hands, keeping the tension a tight rope between over-stimulation, and eternity…

Erin can feel his fingers on her ears, the side of her face. There in that moment there is no cancer, no pain, no grief, no remorse, if God is where two or more are together in my name… She isn't sure if that's blasphemous, but she hopes not… She hopes Mike is thinking the same thing, as his hands travel her body, he can travel her nipples, and her armpits without twitching spasm from within…

then Mike hits her spot in that moment, and it is like a huge cathedral bell is ringing, it is like Spanish moss and live oaks... He touches her clit and more cathedral bells ringing in eternity, a vibration like a sonnet, that beautiful rainy day when they went out to the Springs, and went swimming... In that moment she feels no longing, like Mike and her are sharing one breath... cathedral bells, coming from inside her, and it is the first time Mike ever tried to kiss her in that self-conscious way he does... As she cums she feels that vibration purr and hum through her being...

Afterwards, Mike goes to take a shower, and before he is undressed, she Erin yells," Mike Love," Erin yells, "would you mind running me to see the doctor at Five-thirty. My car is in Bill's shop..."

"What were you saying, hon?," Mike asked entering the room to walk over toward her...
"I got a Doctor's appointment, and was wondering if you'd give me a ride..." Erin said, but she could see his posture change... It was like he knew immediately something was up, she saw his tell, and...
"Are you okay?" He asked...
"Yeah, babe," she said non-chalantly, but she knew he knew she was bullshitting, she could see it. Before he could say something she said," I've got cancer."
Mike's arms were around her, and she just moved into them. He was her bear. He was her everything, and she felt she was betraying him by being sick. She was gonna leave him, and he didn't do well with grief. He... Only then she just gave into his embrace, and held on... She didn't want him ever to let go...

The Emergency Broadcast System went off, and Erin could hear that tone from the other room.

A voice said, "This is not a test. This is a warning the following counties are under a state of Martial Law and Quarantine for the next 72 Hours… Do NOT attempt to leave your homes…"

The voice then goes off to list their county, along with dozens of others… It wasn't even just Florida, but throughout the country from the sound of it. Mike and Erin both sat up a little straighter, but Mike didn't let go of her. She could almost hear him thinking, "what the fuck do I care… Erin's got cancer." He appeared absolutely calm as an announcer started speaking, the words also dancing across the lower portion of the screen…

"Again, The following counties are now under a state of quarantine, and martial law… Effective immediately. All citizens are to stay in your homes… Do not allow others into your homes. The virus responsible is extremely contagious. Carriers of the Virus become extremely aggressive, attacking friends and family, and often they do not seem to recognize anyone… even close families. If you or someone else are sick… try to isolate yourself from them, and call the number on the screen. We will send people to you… Also, We need volunteers".

At this point, several phone numbers came up on the screen for volunteers. They didn't list a number for if people were sick…

"Again, the virus is most likely to be transmitted by exposure to bodily fluid: blood, saliva, etc. It is for this reason, we encourage people to be especially careful about

Dead Man's Kitchen

washing their hands frequently. Again, this is a highly infectious biological agent. Avoid physical contact with those who are sick…

Local healthcare facilities are not able to keep up with the numbers, and we have already had to temporarily close several facilities throughout the South-East due to rioting, and fire… We are working to rebuild and stabilize infrastructure, so we can get those hospitals as quickly as possible, but we need your help…
Stay in your homes… " and the message repeated, again and again…

Mike turns off the television.

CHAPTER 9
Sauchiehall Street
Glasgow, Scotland
Nov. 18, 2013

The city was overrun with a new strain of avian flu. It was airborne, highly contagious, and left a swath of sick it its path. Jordie listened to the news, and was glad that it wasn't Ebola, even if people were dying. The news reported that the Americas had seen an outbreak of a mutated strain of the disease that caused extreme aggression. Other news outlets claimed that it was zombie, vampire, or aliens. Jordie had been reading about the refugees arriving from Sierra Leone on the coast of Italy, and parts of Spain out of Morroco...

The rumors were that people were dying and coming back. Feral, hungry creatures, things that lived only to consume the living...

The government was advising people stay in their homes. The NHS would be organizing to send people out to people's homes. A number asked for volunteers.

Jordie lived in one of the high flats off Glenavon Road. The neighborhood was known to be a touch dodgey, but only for outsiders looking for trouble. He called around to the lads from his old football team. A few of them were sick, and Jordie knew about others sick in surrounding flats. It was bad. It sounded like half the block was already ill. Those that weren't he had meet him in front of the building.

They would take five cars. Donnan, Gregor, Hamish, Finley and Iain were all driving. Jordie rode with Hamish; he had an old BT van that had been converted to a mobile workshop. He also had all the old telephone equipment for plugging directly in at the box, other equipment he could use to intercept cell phones, long and shortwave radio... Hamish was some super genius who just hung out with a bunch of neds. Yes, they'd all grown up in the same scheme, but any day now Jordie expected to hear that Hamish had joined the SAS or something.

They all showed up dressed in heavy jackets with hoodies, and wore joggie bottoms. Jordie knew that they were the total stereotype of the kind of people who loot stores. They were neds, or yobs; they were seen as trouble by most, but... in a very short time people would go to the Tesco to find it overrun by looters. Right now, there were still groceries on the shelves. He sent Fraser with Emmett, to go after medical supplies, since he'd been a paramedic back in the States. The drug companies tried to make it more difficult to track their operations by changing drug names, but... he was top notch.

The people in each car had a mission: one or two items that they must acquire or not return home. It was like a quest... Donnan's car was to go after meat, cheese, dairy, things that would go bad in the next few weeks if they didn't have enough space in a freezer. Gregor's car was to go after cigarettes and alcohol -- they were not to drink tonight though. Finley was to go after coffee, sugar, and tea; Iain for baby formula, baby food, nappies, and everything else.

They had gone in casually enough, but by the time

Will Leave you...
All choked up.

Orange Lollipops for the Texas Strangler, and... Gutter Punk Noir

Eric "Moebius" Morlin

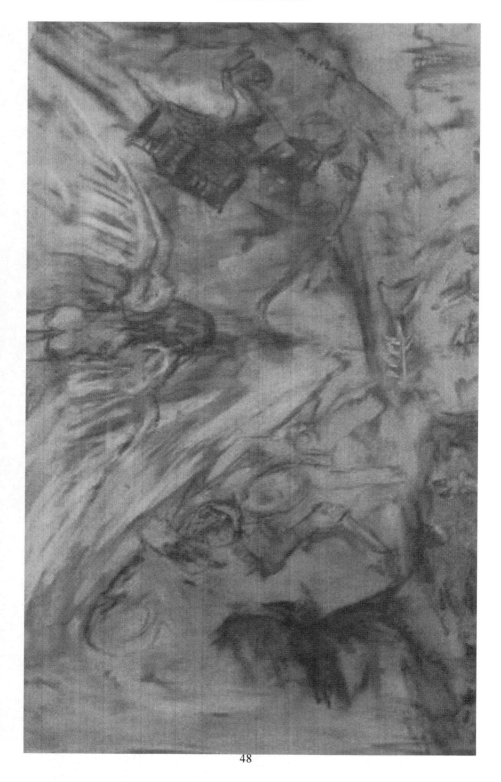

Dead Man's Kitchen

everyone had filled their carts the demeanor of people inside had changed. There was a man out in front of the store snarling and attacking people. A man was yelling to the manager, "I'm telling you that guy bit me… he…"

They went right after him, the girl at the counter not even saying anything. Outside, the manager was fighting off one of those eater things… it was for real. Jordie knew as soon as he saw the guy. He was snapping at the Tesco manager. Jordie took a heavy can from his cart, and smashed the man in the face… The Eater let go of the manager, and fell back; Jordie hit him twice more before he went down.

He didn't get up again.

"You killed him," the manager said. "I saved your arse," Jordie replied.

People would go out to to get groceries in the hours that followed only to find everything was becoming overrun with looters. There were people walking the streets, some who were obviously unwell.

As they piled back into their vehicles, Jordie could see a man coughing up blood, another laying unmoving. He was right, they had timed everything perfectly. An hour later they were standing on the roof of his flat. They could see some kind of crazy riot, with molotovs, and a burning car, but… that was just Maryhill. He loved this city and it was under attack…

Next Jordie had his boys reinforce the doors of the

buildings with plywood. He had people set to guarding all the doors; no one was allowed in if they were bitten... they had enough sick folks in the building already. After a couple supply runs they had enough; they could start putting supplies outside the flats of those who were sick. They would knock on the door from a distance, and then if someone answered, they saw a pallet of water, Dioralyte, Lucozade, Irn Bru... and tins of soup.

The most important thing, according to what he read, was that folks stayed hydrated...

"Those folks are dead already," Iain said.

Jordie nodded. "Probably, but we're better off if they don't... This flu has a 90% mortality rate, but... we know most of these folks. But just in case, none of yous get too close tae them."

Gregor was the last to come back from the latest run... He practically charged through the front door, looking like a fiend, out of breath, soaked with sweat; by the time he'd finally calmed down he was able to get out that the street outside was overrun... He almost didn't make it in, they had to board the front of the building shut, and...

Jordie and the others went out to the rooftop, at first they weren't sure what they were seeing, but then...

There was a huge group of those Eater things, gnawing at Mr. Lewis, a pensioner who lived the next building over. Sure he was a right twat, but... he was their right twat and now his blood and brains were all over the road.

Jordie told the others to grab bats, sticks, anything handy; they need to clear the street of some of this garbage. They went out the side door to the building. It took a lot longer than Jordie would have liked; though the immediate area was clear, he could see more of them slowly filling the street in either direction. Again, he had everyone pile into cars…

The streets were overrun. Hamish was driving. Things looked far calmer from the roof, and Jordie was tempted, even if only momentarily, to tell his crew to go back up, but instead he instead told Hamish to gun it. Hamish tried to avoid the main mass of bodies, but one of them still went up onto the bonnet before bouncing off the windscreen…

"Where we going?" Hamish asked, and Jordie told him, "Kelvingrove… The Museum, it has some kinda armour display, medieval knights an' all that… figure will do a lot better than Cricket bats…"

Outside the Museum was a banner proclaiming the museum's 'Arms and Armour' exhibit is on display. Jordie hadn't been there for some time, he'd thought that he might be able to just drive up and smash the front doors, but he'd forgotten the stairs. They ended up having to take down a lamp to use as a battering ram, and then they were inside.

Alarms went off, but either the guards were all sick, or they could see the large group and decided to wait for backup. The lobby has an old airplane hanging from the rafters, a Spitfire LA198. The armoury takes up the whole top floor. There are rooms full of swords and armor. Ten suits of armour stand tall, including one armored knight on horseback. The young men all started grabbing weapons, Finley started to put on armor. Jordie says, "You might wait on that…"

Finley looked at Jordie puzzled, and Jordie replied, "you'll have a hard time fitting into your car… maybe the gauntlets, and whatever they call those things for your arms… eventually, sure… but we just don't have time."

Finley hauled a huge armored mannequin, as did a couple of others… Jordie thought to himself that it was taking longer than he'd like, and yelled for the others to, "Load up…" He realized now they need a truck, or several…

Iain gathered together all the black powder weapons.

When they got to the front of the building they could see a few eaters coming up the hill, most likely attracted by the alarm. The weapons were heavy, but served their purpose… they dispatched the eaters quickly before loading everything.

Jordie knew he needed to see the bigger picture, or the city would devour them.

Hope gives us something to work with…

Chapter 10
Saved by the Dead man
November 19, 2013

In some ways, what happened in the subway in Yokohama was devastating, as it led to the fall of the current Japanese government, but it also led to a city able to survive such an upheaval. After the subway, the eaters were quickly able to overtake half the city…

It is only because of the sheer persistence of the people that they were able to close off the subways. The martial arts community was invaluable in assisting in the isolation and capture of tens of thousands of sick citizens.

In other cities, local member organizations of the Budokhan gather students to be on the local for persons showing symptoms to help quarantine them. This has allowed Japan the ability to rescue far larger number of their population than any other civilized nation. This isn't to say that the Nipponese did not lose cities to the eaters, but their ability to organize has at least temporarily granted them a reprieve from the fate of the rest of the world.

Keeping up with food production, has been a struggle, and led to nationwide rationing.

Chapter 11
Just beyond Sunspot
Cloudcroft, NM
Nov 22, 2013

The outbreak first started a little over a week ago, and while most of the folks up in the mountains are good about keeping extra supplies… Already people are starting to ration themselves.

A year ago, Caleb Marshall had started his bid to buy out the German Airforce in Alamogordo. The end was near, and had planned to have the purchase completed by 2020, but with the benefit… he figured out a way to maintain the political sovereignty. Only, now… The weapons contractor was thinking, he might now need any of that… He had established his corporate headquarters at Sunspot only 3 short months ago…

When the plague had first hit he'd recommended they blow the tunnel going down into Alamo, but people had rejected the idea… Only earlier this evening a group of soldiers been discovered looting a farmhouse, near High Rolls. The soldiers killed. Their equipment confiscated, but… everyone knew this would mean a whole lot of trouble from down the hill.

So it was, that the people met up in town for a city council session, that me miners blow the tunnel while the meeting is in session. The town seems relatively free of undead so far, but supplies are beginning to dwindle. People talk of consolidating resources, whereupon Marshall announces… "I've got a lot of supplies. I can't feed everyone in town by any means, but I've got enough to feed about 25 people for the next year…" he didn't mention this didn't include feeding his own people, or that it didn't actually even take a dent out of his supplies…

"but there are things I need... Things and skill sets I do not possess, if we are to continue...." That is when the tunnel blows... Agreeing to feed so many people took their attention from looking further into what Marshall had back at Sun spot...

CHAPTER 12
<u>Old Hewlitt's Sawmill</u>
Serepta, Ms
Nov. 23, 2013

The building for the old Sawmill didn't even exist, but the homestead still existed. There were 3 houses on the property, and numerous outbuildings, but the place was empty. Henry had been out with Jason all afternoon, scavenging. Country folks as a rule, aren't as wasteful. Which means if someone else didn't get there first… They parked behind the main house on the property, an old brick house, and then went to bang on the front door.

"Someone is inside…," Henry started to say, but then… he knew whomever the owner might have been, it was not the current occupant.

"What?" Jason says, in a drawl, that he's thrown on extra thick…

"Shut up, and let's get inside," Henry says, and opens the door. An old woman in a night gown, which is torn and covered in blood. It looks like it was probably a really pretty green once. She comes through the doorway quickly, but Jason already has his bayonet in front of him. He's using an old Mauser rifle, that belonged to his grandpa.

They managed to find a ton of canned goods. A couple dozen chickens out back. The power grid had just died earlier in the day… so everything in the deep freeze appeared to be still frozen. It was mostly full of Venison, and beef, and a turkey. Jason only just remembered it was Thanksgiving… They'd have to do something special for the kids. They took the whole deep freeze and loaded it onto the truck. They loaded up all of the Chickens. Whereupon there realized there were a lot more animals at behind the next house over...

The next house over had been kept immaculately. They had to break down the doors to get in, using a wagon axle as a battering ram. The owners appeared to have committed suicide. Although, the house was fully stocked... like these folks had been preparing for it for decades. The family had owned a Diesel Suburban, which they had totally full of tools, welding gear, reloading equipment, ammo, weapons, and MRE's. The house was no way near stripped. However, by the time they'd got two horse trailers attached, and the animals out of the barn it was already starting to get dark.

As the got to Henry's place they saw where old man Calhoun was parked out front. They were also two eaters down by the fence. Calhoun lives on a nearby farm with his wife, and kids who returned from college when the plague first broke out.

"Hey Henry, I just wanted to tell you to be careful... Last night around 7pm someone shot one of my horses," Calhoun says.

Sadly, I know who the more likely culprit is... and then I hear him speak up.

"Someone shot your horse?" Jason asks.

Calhoun turns, and says, "Yes! I was inside when I heard the shot. It's a good thing I heard too, was able to butcher it and save all the meat... Can't afford to let food go to waste right now..."

"That's for dang sure," Jason replies. They all talk a little while longer, before Calhoun drives off into the night.

"You killed that man's horse, didn't you?" Henry asks, and Jason laughs, and says, "I might of... I shot at me a deer out that way, about the same time... He got away, but... maybe the bullet carried..."

"You shot the man's horse?!" Henry says incredulously!

Dead Man's Kitchen

"I didn't mean to, I swear," Jason says, and, "I make it up to him…"
"Now don't go swearing. And Calhoun probably already knows… was probably why he came by… So you need to make it up to him somehow, but don't tell him you did it, or he'll make you owe him a new herd…"Henry responds.
"Seriously," Jason asks.
"as a dead horse, in a time of famine," Henry replies.

The power grid had stayed up and running at the house for almost a week, and then yesterday it died. Henry had been ready for it. He didn't need a lot of electricity anyways. They kept the fridge and deep freeze going, and chargers for flashlights, night vision goggles and such, but mostly they tried to ration their gas until they could find more, which they had achieved when Jason acquired a tanker truck full of gas. Jason had his CDL, and that was proving more useful now than ever before.
There were things they still needed to find a source for, they had quite the surplus of most things, but things like toilet paper only lasted so long, and Henry had to admit he'd become spoiled. See Henry was part of that generation that used corn cobs, and Fig leaves, and he didn't really want to go back. It was a good way to get chiggers on your peckerwood, not to mention ticks, and everything else…
However, they had enough to last for a while, and they had cows, chickens, and other animals. Which wasn't the case for everyone. This also made them a target, but since Jason arrive they'd had a few other untimely arrivals… Some relatives who, just remembered they once had lived outside

a city, Injun Fellah name Freud who used to live on the Rez in Oklahoma… What with Tammy's kids their number was hitting 23.
Freud was a decent enough sniper, and Jason could shoot you dead if you were on a horse. So they had it covered.

What few conveniences they lacked were things like butter, mayonnaise, sour cream, all that stuff that tastes great but is awful for you. Henry loved his butter, so he taught the young un's how to make it.

****

Butter

What you need:
two mason jars
full of fresh cream
that's it really…

Directions:
Shake the mason jars full of cream, and keep at it, after a while the cream will start to congeal and clot inside the jars; That's butter you're making.
The longer you shake it, the more it will separate out, until you have one big hunk of butter in each jar, and some liquid.
If you like butter milk you can drink the liquid, if not you can use it to make biscuits, or add it to your slop bucket to feed your dogs.

CHAPTER 13
Rain through the Ceiling

Casselberry, FL
Nov 25, 2013

Elsie was scavenging by herself in a grocery store in Casselberry, a shitty neighborhood before the end of the world. Actually it might be less sketchy now...

She had been in the store under 5 minutes. The store had been stripped of anything a person might want to eat. This isn't to say it was empty, even though the looters had taken most everything including the cash register... Which amused Elsie at the time. How far had they carried a worthless cash register and its contents.

All the meat was gone, thankfully though the place still smelled of those few odd bits of produce that got missed, or had fallen behind something, meat, cheese, eggs all gone, no coffee... they missed a bag of sugar though, though...

Major score!

The door to the store had opened then... three young guys. Elsie had thought there would be trouble, then guy in front smiled. He had red hair and freckles, and looked totally harmless in those moments. "Hey! Oh, my God another person," he said with a smile, "I'm Rudy..."

He opened his arms, hugged her. She'd hugged all of them in fact. They'd helped her look through the store… managed to find a flat of cream corn, a couple cans of asparagus, jar of olives, and two boxes of Graham crackers. As they chatted about the world as it had been. She'd told them about her boyfriend. How he'd gotten bitten at the Veterinarian hospital where he'd worked, by another person. They'd talked about past girlfriends, but it was all before folks got sick. They had lost family, friends, but no lovers. They all sounded strangely chaste, as they helped her carry the food to her Subaru. Some eaters were slowly beginning to drift toward the front of the building, but they'd talked her into one last run.

Now that she thought about it, most of the other markets she'd searched had eaters out front. They'd gone to search the back of the store. The place had smelled like mildew, and rotten food. When "Surprise," one of them was on her back, had her in a choke hold and taken her down to the ground with him. Rudy took her gun, even now his smile looked innocent. When she was down on the ground, she saw that it was the one who'd called himself Clint behind her. Clint who she'd hugged, and talked to about his grandmother who lived in Apopka. The one who'd told her his name was Greg was between her legs, pulling her blue jeans down, when Clint let up on the choke, She screamed, screamed looking down to see…

There were many thoughts going through her head all at once, including a part of her brain that was laughing hysterically. It made fun of everything and everyone, and then tried to rationalize her out of it. Then, Why does this idiot think he has to rape someone? He's got an average

Dead Man's Kitchen

penis. They were all cute, funny... What is wrong with these guy? What is wrong with them?," she thought and even... thought about taunting Greg in her final moments, then, "but they might let me... live... "

She screamed... like there was anyone out there who might hear her other than eaters... That was what these men were too, eaters. Maybe not all men, or all women, all people when she let her be honest. She thought of her dead boyfriend. They were taking some time apart.

"Let me get in there," Rudy said, acting like he was trying to push Greg out of the way, and her pants coming down a little bit more... he was laughing. They were laughing and inside her head.. So was she, not cause she was happy for certain, but laughing hysterically at herself, at this screwed up situation, at these idiots jerk douche bag losers... and then she'd felt it... Clint had a gun strapped to his ankle, "Oh, God help me get out of this... Just got to pace myself..." She screamed hoping she could shatter every fucking window in the place. She screamed like it might be the only chance...

"Dang it Jeff, Shut her the Hell..." Greg started to say to Clint before his head exploded against the wall. He was still holding on to the sides of her blue jeans, and her panties... His body fell back. With her pants, and panties down to her knees she went for Jeff/ Clint's gun, and shot him dead on in the café muscle. He shriek worse that she did... She shot at Rudy. So did someone else, but he dove... One of them got him. She could see blood. She started to run, but remembered her pants... as if you can forget you've got a dead guy pulling your pants down. Only Jeff/ Clint had grabbed the back of her leather jacket. She turned and fired. "Ahhh ha ha," He screamed, almost like he was laughing too... and then Elsie was moving, away from Rudy, and Jeff/Clint, and toward the shooters.

Hoping, no... praying that she wasn't running into some bigger helping of stupid from the universe.

She broke free from headless, in more ways than one, Greg... and ran, as well as one can with their pants and panties down to their knees, trying to yank them up simultaneously. Finally, she just stopped, right in the middle of everything. There were bullets flying around everywhere, and time was on slow mo as she started to hike up her britches... tugged on her blue jeans... She had to put the revolver she'd taken from Clint/Jeff into the crotch of her blue jeans in order to use both hand, then before she could get them all the way up, reach down to put it in the back of her blue jean... She finished yanking 'em up, and turned, fired a bunch of wild shots, and then ran...

right into the girls...

Tanya, and Talesha, although they didn't actually introduce themselves to her 'til later. Right then people were shooting at each other, and... "Get down, girl," Tanya says to her. The girls have got plenty of cover behind the wall of the old walking cooler. Rudy and the others are cowering behind some an old forklift, and some other junk. The gun fight didn't continue another minute before Jeff/ Clint says, " Stop shooting... We ... C'mon Rudy I been gut shot..."

"You ladies are wasting all your bullets, and you can be sure those things hear us," Rudy says.

"I ain't in no hurry," Tanya says, "You in a hurry?"

No one fires for a minute, then Rudy says, "We're almost outta bullets..."

"Awesome, that will certainly make this easier," Talesha says.

"Can we surrender, so my buddy don't die..." Rudy asks.

Dead Man's Kitchen

"You can," Tanya says, "Throw out your guns…"

"I'm viscous, but I'm not stupid. I do that, you'll just kill us," Rudy says.

"Look you meat head… I said I wouldn't kill you if you throw out your guns, and you want to imply I'm a liar, and I'm lying to you… You are certainly stupid. However, I told you something, and I stand by my guns… You throw out your guns, and I won't kill you… but I'm losing my patience."

The guns were thrown out into the open.

"Tallie," Tanya says, signaling to her friend.

"What?" She responded.

"Get their guns," Tanya said.

"Why can't you get 'em. You're the one negotiating with these little…"Talesha starts to say, and suddenly Elsie is laughing hysterically. Talesha looks behind her and then, goes to get the guns. After she walks back over…

Tanya says," Now stand up."

"Hell no," Rudy responds, as Clint/Jeff his fellow piece of human garbage groans in agony.

"DO it NOW," Tanya says. Rudy hesitates a few seconds more, then stands with his arms up over his head. Clint/Jeff ain't going no where…

"You gonna kill me now," Rudy asks.

"Are you dead yet, moron?" She replies.

Rudy shakes his head….

"Then Shut up," the girls both say in unison. Afterwards they have him raise his shirt and turn in place…

"Oh, I see… checking out the merchandi," Rudy starts to say, but is interrupted by the sound of Talesha making puking noises. She turns to walk out of the store, Elsie follows quickly after…

"Ha ha," Rudy says smarmily, "You took our fing

Eric "Moebius" Morlin

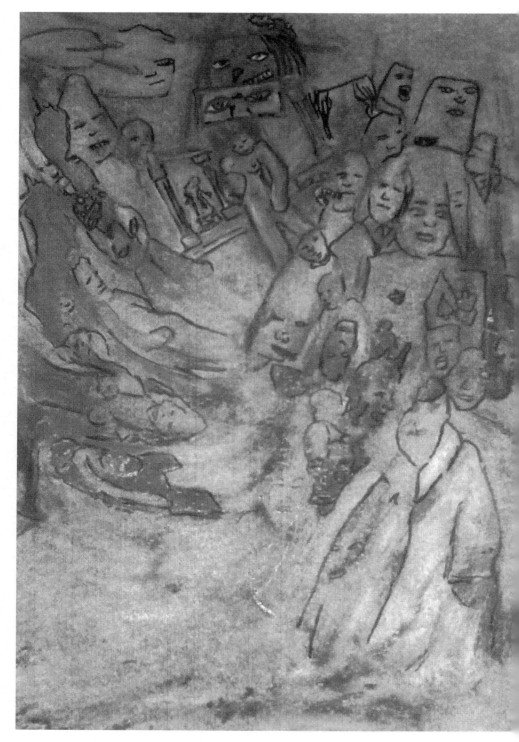

Dead Man's Kitchen

weapons. You might as well have left us, for dead... Heck you're fucking us worse than we did your stupid frien..." and then he pauses, realizing he might have pushed it a little too far...

Tanya continues to point the gun at him, and says, "not entirely accurate," and shoots Rudy in the knee cap, saying," Cause you and your friends didn't fuck no body with those baby dicks of yours... "

Rudy is screaming now, "You lying whore... You fucking killed me..."

"And I just fucked you way harder and deeper," Tanya says," my dick is way bigger..."

She turns and walks out of the room, Rudy howling after her... Talesha and Elsie are waiting by the door. There are a few eaters close by, and the girls kill shoot the closest, but... Tanya also leaves the door to the grocery store wide open. They pile into Laura's Subaru, and she drives South...

"Oh, by the way," Tanya says, "My name is Tanya... and this is Talesha."

"oh... Thank you for saving I'm Laura," Elsie says.

"my friends call me Tallie,"Talesha says.

"Nice to meet you Laura, and... I just realized," Tanya holds up a cell phone showing the date, "Only three days to Thanksgiving..."

The car goes quiet after that. Elsie moves as if she is about to turn off the radio, then stops, and laughs as she puts her other hand back on the wheel. There were crowds of them hanging out by the road... not nearly as many as came out at night...

Occasionally they see crowds of eaters, or even other humans... on foot, running and firing at someone or...

Dead Man's Kitchen

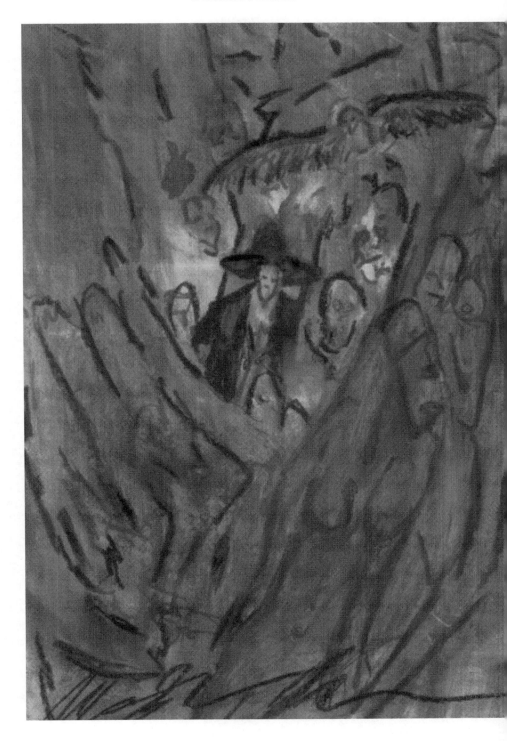

something… Tallie started looking for people she knew in the faces that flashed by… She did it any time she and Tanya drove around together. Today she kept quiet. She had already seen the other girl, Elsie, act crazy. She didn't need to have her thinking… she was crazy too.… then she sees… "Jerry Garcia", she says aloud.

They drive past the blur of a eater standing by the road. It startles, Elsie out of whatever thoughts she'd been in, "What?" She asks half looking at the road for a moment…

Tanya interrupts, "Ignore her. She's playing some celebrity game she saw in a movie… "

Elsie is, like," huh?"

"I was just saying, that dead guy looked like Jerry Garcia," Tallie says.

"Oh, "Elsie says, then laughs… It sounds natural to laugh, and other crowd of gaunt bodies, One an old guy who looks like, "That hair… "Laugh points. "Einstein, "Tanya says. A group of eaters dressed in fatigues are tearing into a man like a lion into an antelope, one eater has biten right into top of the guys shoulder. He has already stopped thrashing beneath them. Then… nothing for a while, then… A doctor, in his surgical scrubs and covered in bite marks is walking across the street with a woman. They are holding hands as they pass in front of Laura's car. She hits the brakes, and the eaters continue across the street as if they'd been on a date…

"Did you guys see that," She starts to ask, and then she sees others coming from out of the nearby woods. She hits the accelerator, and hits an eater. He rolls over the hood, cracking the wind shield where the skull it. The crack is barely the size of a quarter…

"What the," Tanya says. They all look back, even Elsie through the rear view mirror.

Elsie says, "They're still running after the car… So we

know they were eaters, but that couple… "
Tallie says, "maybe they're doing the cover yourself with corpse pheromone, and act like you're dead, and know what you're doing… method. Ha"
Firemen, fast food guy, hairdresser, guy in gorilla suit… It is like the world's biggest street party, except no one made it to the party alive… There's a woman in a bright blue dress, standing there in the middle of the road…. She is missing an ear, and part of her face, but the dress is spotless.
"Some kinda blue sequins," Elsie says," It looks like she just died… "
"there is no reason a dead woman's dress should look that,"Tallie starts to say, before, Elsie starts to do a u-turn. "What are you…"Tanya and Talesha start to say in unison.
"I'm gonna run over that bitch," Elsie says.
When they get past the woman, and the next median, she u-turns again… There she is standing in the road ahead of them, only now she is facing away from the road. Elsie hits her anyway. When the woman starts to get back up Elsie backs over her several times, and…
"I cannot believe it," She says…
The dead woman in the blue dress lies in front of them on the road. The treads have torn into her skull, a piece of tibia juts out of her right leg.
"what?" Tanya asks…
She jumps out the Subaru, and… "What the hell is she doing?" Talesha asks. The girls see Elsie lift up the dead woman by the hair, and then return to the car… "What did you just…do?" Tallie ask. "Oh, I looked at the label on her dress, that material is incredible. Gonna track down the manufacturer," Elsie says.
"I say this, in the nicest way… You're a crazy bitch," Talesha says.

Dead Man's Kitchen

Eric "Moebius" Morlin

Elsie laughs. If she survived she wanted to redesign civilian to

They are quiet again for a while… Almost all the roads are blocked at the major intersections on Colonial drive. "Are we going someplace in particular," Tallie asks.

"Huh? What…" Elsie says, "I'm sorry I…"

"No, I get it… You've been through a lot, I get it Tanya responds," I was just asking if we're going someplace in particular…"

"oh, yes… I have a… house," Elsie tells them, "but… it's in really, really bad shape, Just…the word dump doesn't do the place justice." She laughs then, and says," um… You guys are going to thing I'm really crazy when you see the place…"

Tanya bites her teeth together at this thought, and hopes it isn't the case…

Tallie looks up to see a town named Bithlo, and thinks famous for the race track, and… meth labs.

"Whew," she thinks… her teeth don't look bad, "Just hope it ain't that…"

They make several turns off Colonial, so now only Elsie knows where they're at… She pulls into a drive way, pushes the clicker on her garage door opener, and…

"this place looks decent…"Tanya says," Quiet neighborhood…? And there's still power?"

"Yeah, but this isn't where we're staying… oh, and the garage door opener is connected to a deep cycle battery. She closes the garage with them in it. Turns off the car and begins to take the battery out. This she switches with a battery sitting on one of the shelves. She places the other battery in the car.

"Clever, so no one will steal your car without their own

battery, if they don't figure out the garage door has power too," Tallie says.

"They won't from here," She pushes a wall button, and the garage door stays still," I broke the switch so it only opens with this thing…" Holding the garage door opener. They proceed to load up their packs with the supplies, and Elsie guides them through the house. This is the kitchen, living room, that's a bathroom. It has water in the tank. If you use it… refill it. There's water in the tub. This is the master bed room. She shows them a release for a door…

"My parent's used to live here, that's why I know.." Elsie becomes silent, and leads them out a door in the back yard.

It is fenced in, and the gate is closed. At some point, neither girl sees when, Elsie acquires a machete that was stuck in a tree in the back yard. The girls have their guns out, as they go over a fence, and into the woods behind the house.

The walk in silence for a while, only occasionally stopping to listen…

"So, you used to play in these woods as a kid or something,"Tallie asks.

"Yeah," Elsie replies.

The walk for what feels must be a mile or more, when Elsie signals them to stop. She then goes into the woods to where some orange trees are growing wild… She offers the fruit to both girls. Tanya refuses, saying she doesn't eat citrus. "Well, I hope you're taking vitamin C then, cause it is either that, or scurvy, and that's some bad shit," Elsie says," I mean, it takes months, but… consider… before you were getting a balance meal, maybe a multi vitamin… "

"So what happens if I don't," Tanya asks.

"um… let's see, body won't produce collagen the way it should, problems with iron absorption which I'm sure you know binds to oxygen in our blood… It can cause ulcers in

Dead Man's Kitchen

your mouth, loss of teeth, edema, exhaustion, anemia, debility... women who have it when pregnant have children whose brain doesn't develop properly... it's bad stuff..."Elsie says.

Tanya and Talesha both laugh. "Were you a nurse, or a Doctor, or something," Tallie asks.

"Massage therapist," Elsie replies...

"Really!" Tanya says, rubbing her neck, "I could use a massage. What do you charge?"

They laugh, Tanya ends up taking an orange, and then Tallie says," Seriously, though, how the hell far are we going..."

Elsie points and says," see that ditch way up there?"

"Barely," Tallie says.

"That's half way," Elsie says.

Tallie lets out a groan, and they all shoulder their packs

again. Finally they see a house off in the distance. There are several large out buildings as well.

"Walk where I do, from here on out," Elsie says.

"You set booby traps?" Tanya asks.

"My uncle did," Elsie she says in a voice just above a whisper.

"Was that his house," Tanya asks.

"Oh, no, this place is old Florida... I just stumbled into it... I don't think anyone else even knows it exists, besides us," She replies.

"You just said your uncle..."Tallie interrupts.

"Set the traps. Yes, he did, but that was before," Elsie points around her, as she says," everything, you know," She pauses... and for a moment she tightens the muscles of her face, and then, continues speaking," before everything went and got crazier than it already was... He used to rent this house by exchanging working on it... "

The girls are having a hard time seeing what the girl's father might have done....

As the approach the main house, they can already see a pool enclosure has been added on to the older Florida home. The house looked huge, old Spanish.

"Pool," Tallie asks.

Elsie responds," Yeah, it's saltwater, but right now it looks pretty bad... intentionally, but...

The inside of the house has looks bad unintentionally... at least on my part."

As they get closer, the girls can see the pool enclosure is covered in debris, and has huge tears in places.. The roof of the house looks like someone had attempted to tarp it and failed...

The pool looked frightening, green, and there were things swimming in it...

Inside the house it was like a maze made out of horded

goods. There was a huge hole in the ceiling about 4 feet and a tube on the floor beneath it... In the other rooms are more tubs, and a large fish aquarium. Each looks to be full of rain water...

"You have a lovely home," Talesha says, there is no hint of sarcasm or humor.

"I appreciate the words, and... I get that this is bad..." She puts her hand on Talesha's shoulder, and says, "you don't want to go to that part of the house... It makes this part of the house look nice... not to mention floors caving in in places, and... I relocated the previous owners creepy video collection into that part of the house. Elsie shudders.

She walks them past the kitchen, and up a decaying stairway, into an open room, and... Elsie walks across the room to where there is a dresser in on corner, she goes behind the dresser and... in between a gap between where the two walls meet. It was in no way obvious. The girls followed cautiously, as the narrow hall opens into what at first appears to be a closet, but then Elsie does something to open a door, where there once was a shelf... and they can feel all feel the cool of air conditioner. The two girls

start to push themselves and Elsie into the next room.

"Oh, wow," Tanya says, and the room is... nothing like the rest of the house. There are no holes in the ceiling, no buckets of rain, no mildew smell. Elsie points to the bathroom, a huge walk in closet that seems full up with supplies.

"Why the hell were you scavenging? You've got enough there to keep you for a year or more,"Tallie asks. "There's enough for about 8 people for a year," Elsie said," and I didn't want to share it alone... My uncle, mom, dad, my boyfriend, their all dead… I decided I had to get out… wasn't thinking, didn't even grab a gun. My dad would have been so pissed." Elsie is shaking her head, "Oh, are you guys hungry, because I just found the last thing I need to make a couple lemon Iced box pies.

This is her recipe.
****

LEMON Iced box Pie
(makes 2 small pies or 1 large one)

2 Cans Eagle Brand Condensed Milk
6 egg yolks (beat)(RESERVE WHITES FOR TOPPING)
1 Cup Lemon (can substitute Lime Juice)
1 teaspoon Lemon or Lime Zest (optional)

Mix well and pour into 2 graham crust or 1 large graham cracker crust. We make our own crusts (by adding graham crackers, about 1 or 2 tablespoons butter and a little sugar-- for crust--crush all this together and press into pie plate) or you can buy your own graham cracker crust.

TOPPING
6 egg whites
1 teaspoon vanilla flavoring (optional)
6 teaspoon sugar(taste for sweetness)

Beat egg whites, sugar until stiff.
Bake 350 degrees until golden brown(watch carefully).

Dead Man's Kitchen

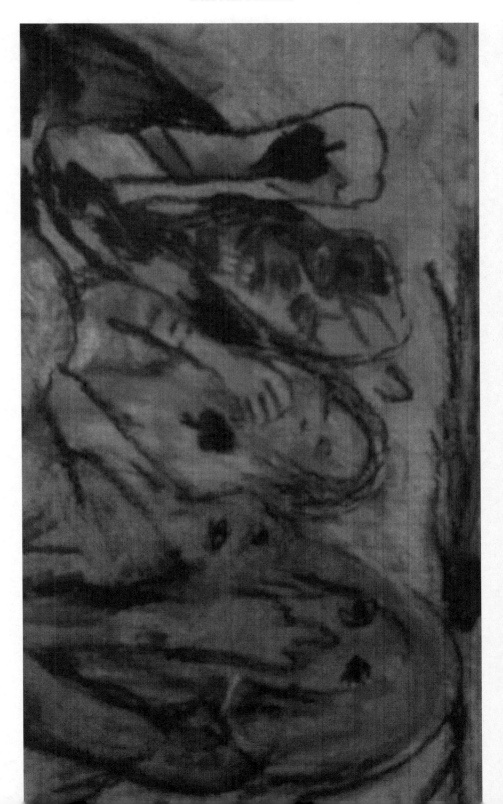

Chapter 14
Heart of Darkness
Lagos, Nigeria
Dec 7, 2013

Tom Warner had lived in Nigeria since the '80's. He worked for Westerhouse back then, trying to get Nitel up and running... It was a dreadful place back then... Every Sunday the television would show people being taken out to the beach, tied to a post and shot... Not even kidding.

It was Firing Squad Sunday.

It was a ruthless place. If you stole from someone... they would trap you and a wrap your living body in tires, and douse you in gasoline, and set you on fire...

Lately it had gotten even crazier... They didn't go out of their compound anymore. At first they'd thought it was just Ebola, and that was bad enough... Watching people bleed from their eyes and ears, mouth, watching the skin slough away on them, but then to see this ulcerous thing running full out at one of your mates, and jump on him... it... made one hesitate.

Nigeria has been a place full of death since Tom arrived, but now the sky is so thick with flies they look like a dense fog. Those dead that don't return are food for maggots, but the insects don't discriminate, and slowly they eat the eaters as well.

People have since come to terms with the fact that it wasn't Ebola, MERS, or SARS making everyone crazy, but the very act of dying, and those dead were out screaming on the streets. The city had almost a million people, but now there seemed to be more than a million dead devouring everything like locusts.

So, they kept inside, kept their heads down, and the windows covered… business as usual in Nigeria, really… but why the heck Tom had stayed so long he still couldn't tell you. Yeah, the money was good, but now days it was paying way better to go to Iraq, or Afghanistan… He'd just stayed too long.

There had been almost 50 people working at the Westerhouse compound before the outbreak. This number had been reduced to 37, though 18 had actually died. The additions were two Nigerian children, a girl named Mali (9), and a boy named Christoph (11). The children had been runners for the people in the compound before the sickness, and now more than ever.

The children had shown up one night when things were especially bad outside. Mark Waller had been watching the front gate with Jack Bennet and Pat Jainee. Jack had wanted to leave the children to the eaters, but Mark and Pat had vetoed him.

He'd complained that it was just one more mouth to feed, though the two children together ate less than any one person on rations, and since they'd arrive they had managed to scavenge enough to feed Mark's fat ass, ten times over…

The other new members were actually familiar faces as well. Charles and Reggie were brothers, and they had worked as intermediaries between the company and the government for the last ten years that Tom had been here. The other was Gerald Finey, he was a native African, of Dutch descent. He'd been born in South Africa but had been working for Aero Contractors for the last three years. The Aero Contractors compound had gotten over last week, and it looked like he was the only one to have survived.

When Tom first moved here, they'd come in on Pan Am. Now, Pan am was out of business, and nobody was flying into Lagos, or… taking connecting flights out of anywhere in Northern Africa. South Africa wasn't faring much better. Now… there was nowhere to fly too, which had been considered since… Gerald had been an Airframe Power plant guy back at the Aero Contractors compound… so if they could find a plane, he might be able to get it up and running… The problem is they were still trying to figure out if there was someplace to fly too… Only this was still circumvented by their biggest problem, finding a pilot, and not getting into a show down as they tried to flee the country…

They had a fair surplus of food, just because Westerhouse's main distribution warehouse was right in their compound… However, over the last week the Nigerian military had been sniffing around, a lot… and if they got any idea of what was inside that compound..

Finally they'd been able to talk to General Mahonbe. He'd been a guard at the compound previously, and it seems… He had been pivotal in leading the Coup. It had helped to have a crippling plague ravaged the country, but… no one was sure there would still be a country in the coming months. He called us on our satellite phone, and said he would like to come out and visit us…

This could be dangerous for us, because once his men were

through the front gate of our compound they could decide it was nicer that "what they have at home," as it were... but it might be our best chance at survival.

Mahonbe arrives the next morning outside the gates at 9 a.m. sharp, plowing a path through the bodies of eater, and non-eaters alike if they were foolish enough to get in the way. Our men fired flame throwers down onto some of the eaters, to help clear the path, but Manhonbe's men didn't even slow. I guess they knew the capabilities of their military transport... The vehicles they drove were almost too tall for the gates... Almost like large armored RV's, ...
We got the gate open just in time for Manhonbe's Clavacade to come through, as we closed the gates behind them, we have a vehicle alongside it... Once it was in place the gate might even be able to resist one of Manhonbe's armored trucks, but before that it was vulnerable to being pushed off track....

Chapter 15
Day of the Dead

Mexico City, Mexico
Dec 8, 2013

A city of nearly 7 million dead... The eaters run the streets prowling hungrily, and most of the residents who have survived stay in their homes.

The northern part of the city is on fire, and has been for almost a week... The fire had started with a gas line, though no one knew if it had been intentional or not. Afterwards the house caught blaze, and leapt over to a neighboring apartment building. There living and dead toppled from the balconies. As with a game of dominoes the fire spread from home to house, to cars, gas stations... The blaze consumed the city relentless, and those who could flee went North. The fire continued as if pursuing them into the countryside...

Eaters often seem to dance along the perimeter of the blaze... Others would use the age old metaphor, of moths flying to close to the flame, but often here... the dead would catch fire, and slow dance piroting in a Macabre downward spiral...

It is the hottest December on record, even the zombies appear to be sweating as blood runs down their faces... but no one brings up the issue of global warming.

Lorenzo, and Oscar Rivas have managed to barricade themselves along with about a dozen others in an old Cathedral. They had considerably more food a month ago, but... now there is a a few cans of beans, and a bag of candy between them. The situation has become desperate enough that they two men have decided to try and create a walkway with some planks that were sitting in the church courtyard... Jorge, an older man, and a boy everyone calls Arturo wait behind on the rooftop. They also have a length of rope.

As Oscar walks over to the other building along that lone stretch of wood, he thinks how the Cathedral has been relatively secure, if it weren't for the lack of sustenance. However, the men are not sure anyone else is coming, and it is better to go now while they have some semblance of strength. The ground far below. The dead are reminiscent of a heavy metal concert he saw many years ago.. as the dead occasionally will get pushed up above the crowd and be swept away as if crowd surfing.

Next Lorenzo goes across, and as he does so he thinks he recognizes a few bodies that once held the souls of friends, now a vessel for endless mad hunger… He contemplates how to free their souls from sickness, or whatever it is that has taken their bodies..

Below them there are bodies that did not change, instead they contort in rigor mortis, or if they are further along in the purification process they bloat with gasses, but within hours the corpses will become riddled with maggots… Here, ants, Beetles, and wasps all look to build their new home as the skin slow starts to turn first blue, then black.

The two men make it to a nearby building, and start to make their way down a set of stairs. The first floor is quiet.. look through the surrounding apartments. They turn the door to the first apartment, but it doesn't open. They continue until they find a door that opens with ease. This would have been consider looking just a short time ago, now the National Police have fled, along with the military.

Just inside the door, the two men stand silent. There is a sour smell here, that neither man can identify… They are both armed. Oscar has a huge knife, Lorenzo had a machete, but he now also takes hold of a cast iron skillet.

The house is quiet, and the door to the apartment just to the side of the kitchen. There are pictures of an older couple. Someone's Tia perhaps? The two men slowly begin pilfering what the can find… They work hard to make no noise.

Actually, the house is has a surprising amount of food, like perhaps the couple left right after events started to get bad leaving everything behind. There were tomatoes on the table, but they have become a feast for mould, and decay. The still can barely care everything between the two of them...

When it is time to leave, they both shoulder their packs and listen... silence. They go back up to the rooftop without seeing anyone, except Jorge. Oscar does not want to climb over the board again. He lets Lorenzo go first, then signals for them to throw the rope. They pull it taut as he climbs onto a near-by hutch that appears to have once been home to pigeons, maybe... He pulls the line taut and knows it isn't sturdy enough for him, and instead sends his pack, back across...

Then goes back into the apartment building. He had not told Lorenzo his plans. Lorenzo was more cautious, and Oscar thought, probably wiser... He goes back down the stairs and proceeds to check doors... There is a door with blood all over the handle, and at the stoop. Perhaps it is superstitious, but he crosses himself and avoids that door...

The next several doors are locked, and Oscar is worried he might have to force one, rather than be stuck out in the open, but after is third try a door knob turns and... oh, the smell is so terrible. He closes the door for a moment debating going to the next. He hopes that because the place smells of rot, nothing is still alive in or undead inside... The apartment is full of the sounds of flies buzzing. Their bodies liter the floor, as he steps into the room. The apartment has the same floor plan, but in the kitchen is the corpse of a pit bull. Oscar is totally frozen for a moment, and... he has never seen any animal change, but doesn't mean... He stabs the animal at the base of the neck through the spine to be certain, and begins his search.

There are still a few things, cans, can opener (not electric)... He no longer has a pack with him, and so places everything on the kitchen table. He then goes to search the rest of the house. In the living room sits the man of the house facing him. He is long dead, a gun hangs from his hand, the back of his head paints the wall behind him.

He finds a backpack, as well as a pair of heavy leather gloves. He doesn't know if the man had been infected, but knows a solid barrier between him and the ichor of the man's consciousness... He wraps the gun in something, and continues to search. He finds a lot of useful stuff, and thinks to himself what a waste... The man could be alive, had he joined them behind the walls of the old cathedral... instead of just meat in a recliner. After he has the pack full, Oscar continues on to the next apartment and the next. It is in the 3rd apartment that he encounters his first eater. She is waiting for him as he opens her door, and charges...

Oscar had still been wearing the thick work gloves, and lucky for him as the eater gets one of his fingers in her mouth but he is able to slide his hand out in time. He pushes his knife into her ear, and it sinks in... she goes still. Only Oscar hears more movement in the back bedroom of the apartment... While it does appear there are more supplies to be had, Oscar decides to return home instead...

Lorenzo, Arturo, and Jorge are still waiting on the roof... He doesn't know how long he has been gone, but... He again sends his pack over first.

Afterwards, he slowly makes his way across the board. He realizes half way across that the rope is within reach if he needs it, but... that seems to be enough to keep his terror at bay.

They all go inside to have dinner.

CHAPTER 16
Deep in the Heart of…
Austin, Tx
Dec 9, 2013

Last month, this time… It was a city of almost 2 million. A lot of guns in Texas. In the first weeks, Austin was almost un touched. Almost as soon as the outbreak occurred, the city Mayor set to up to block all in coming traffic coming into the city.

Outside of the city, the Texas National Guard continue to establish various fortifications around the city, including a kind of cattle guard meant to prevent zombies from walking into the city. However, once they are covered with enough bodies the dead are able to climb over each other.

However, as the state of Texas announced its independence and the formation of a Nation of Texas, "Texas Embassies," have started appearing around the state, especially where persons are trying to enter municipalities for trade, sanctuary, or to be reunited with family. As the great Nation of Texas wanted to encourage people to be more health conscious country, these embassies were usually located near luxury hotels. The guests first having to endure a quarantine process that was packaged as a day of massage therapy, with hot tub, and lazy river.. The process has enabled Texas to stop 230 persons with bites from entering the country. This is of course not including the number of eaters that are prevented from entering various municipalities by use of physical force.

Citizens are encouraged to take their own preventative

measures in the home to put barriers of protection between themselves and loved ones who might be more susceptible to an untimely death. While some have recommended that this isn't done in an overly crude or blatant fashion as it might create feelings of alienation, and discomfort. Others recommend installing In-home gating systems for those with family members age 65 and older in the house.

Additionally, those wishing to enter the state of Texas are being required to show proof of employment in the state, or assisting persons wishing to enter the state in finding work. If they have employment in Texas already it is simplified greatly… If not they were directed to another… Much, much longer line… Unless you want to be a soldier, in which case you were directed to a swearing in ceremony, and given a gun… With almost one person in every house hold a gun owner, and most folks owning 2-5… They had it covered in that department.

However… people now were encouraged to save their brass for Texas, in posters everywhere…
Not everywhere was so lucky…
Around the state people work to build watch towers, much like those forestry rangers used to have, along with the gradual construction of walled in safe zones. It is said there will be a wall around the entire state by the end of 2014, others have said this will occur no early than 2015. Texas seem determined to prevail.

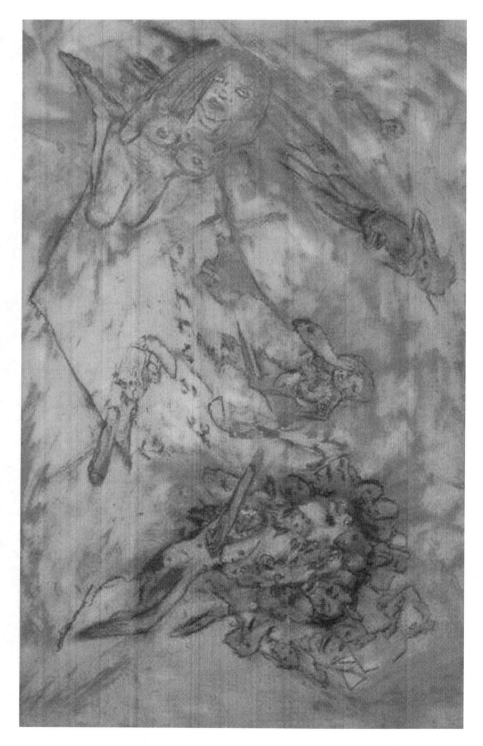

Chapter 17
THE ISLAND
Central Florida
Dec 10, 2013

A guy named Rus Romana asked Mike and Erin to move to Merritt Island and help some folks try to take control of the areas surrounding the bridges into the city.

Rus is an arrogant douche, but he is intelligent, and he offered them supplies in exchange for the help. He said, if they could isolate the city from the main land they might be able to start clearing the rest of the island, but the various strip malls and mall are overrun with eaters. The people who lived there were also dealing with the raider problem. Some of which are selling people into slavery... A hoard of eaters also wandered, and it did not care who it stumbled upon...

Will and the others worked to secure the Farmhouse, which seemed to be possible if they could just figure out a way to camouflage the place, more than by being in a remote part of town... Over the next week Run and Mike's crew blew up Mather's Bridge, isolating the South Most portion of the Island from foot traffic coming North. It seems the military got the same idea taking out bridges at Pineda Causeway (404) into Vierra, 528, and 192... The mainland was cut off, but still Eaters were coming up from the South... A pirate radio station down near Turtle Bay reported eaters had taken over the surrounding countryside around Sebastian, and Indianatlantic. There were, he claimed hundreds of thousands, and they were slowly working their way north.

Other folks on Ham radio, and CB; said these waves of hungry dead were slowly making their way up the coast of Florida... Patrick Air force base, has established a barrier down near Sebastian, beyond that razor wire, and land mines, but once they were over run. It would cost the lives of almost a dozen soldiers, but by using the building of down town Melbourne Beach, along with bulldozers, and rebar palisades… to finally set up a somewhat… "leaky barrier…" where they take out as many eaters each day as they can without getting overrun. They have started to rely more on bladed weapons for the undead, and reserving guns for the living…

The military attempts shang hai recruiting methods for almost a week before the base commander puts it to a stop. The officer who had created the "recruiting program" was executed, along with one of the non-coms… afterwards the military took a more civic minded stance with groups that labeled themselves Militia, neighborhood associations, and one board of realtors…

The rotting organic material had ended up triggering an algae die bloom, and the dead bodies and the dead algae made sure that anyone no one was crazy enough to want to surf in that," Hey Kool aid," moment. Sometimes the living would stumble along with the dead, but with their mind lost with the grief.

It is only 3 months in, and people were only now beginning to realize this isn't anything that is fixed quickly, and people also started to experience their own… blood madness. People who had not been bitten would talk about hearing a call to rage… as if it wasn't just a virus but something in our very blood as a species, as if humanity like an apple was rotting from the inside out…

One night Erin said something about this to Mike, and admitted he felt it too, a strange empathy for sociopathy, feeling like you are in a world run by it, and yet, "here we are saying, from one side of our mouth, how much we feel

Dead Man's Kitchen

Eric "Moebius" Morlin

like we can relate to death… personally, like we just just long lost hungry friends, and we want back into the fold… We want to just give in to become this horrible screaming wave that washes over the world… "

Mike looks up like, "Oh, sorry, just me being crazy."

Only Erin sits up and says," You make it sound… appetizing, you make it almost seem like the right then to do, just give into the hungry feral part of your soul, everyone's gotta die…"Erin says.

"I've always had a problem with romanticizing stupid ugly shit, and making it sound like a good idea… I am just not as good at convincing folks to romanticize good ideas… Also, I said that is what comes out of one side of my mouth…"

"What comes out of the other?" Erin asks, and suddenly she bites at him, a real fierce bite, and Mike rolls away Systema style.

"kisses…"Mike says.

"good boy," Erin replies, and kisses him open mouthed, like cupping water…

After that someone set charges to take out the 528 bridge, and the bridges that led to the space center. "The Island", has become isolated from the mainland for the first time in decades… It is agreed that people make relocate there only if they get checked out first, before the ever cross the river. However, there are three separate groups controlling the boats bringing people over…

A group of ex NASA employees have laid claim Kennedy Space Center since the Federal government ceased to function approximately 2 months ago. A local church group has made a claim to the mall, and is using it to feed homeless. No sermon required. They were getting attacked by raiders for a while, but one of the parishioners, an ex-Marine fellow took over security, and they seem to have stabilized. Rus and Mike are working with the folks that took the city airport.

Lately they've been having a problem with eaters coming out of the nearby rivers, or swamps… It is a constant battle to gain ground, and then… it never seems to stabilize. Erin tries to get Mike interested in going after some slavers that attacked the house they were in… and took two of the girls there. Mike agrees that something must be done, but knows Rus is too self-involved to see the larger picture. He radios to Will and the others that he is coming out before dark.

It is not a good night. They all agree that something must be done, but not necessarily by them…
Mike and Erin only stay the night.

Chapter 18
Purple-ish blue Christmas
Cloudcroft, NM
Dec. 20, 2013

The mountain weather is chilly, a lot of the year, but beautiful... Also, it doesn't seem to agree with the eaters. So... more and more survivors find their way into the mountains. The main problem this creates is with infrastructure, especially... water.

In the weeks that pass Marshall gets his people to negotiate a deal with some folks on the Texas, New Mexico borders to arrange for help acquiring fuel. This allows the town to keep generators running through the Winter. Marshall also helps put together recruiting and scavenging parties to bring back supplies.

They discover whole towns that have been devoured whole. In some the people were murdered obviously by raiders, at other times... where the dead have taken residence.

The school and hotel both began to fill up with new residents, and a program is established so that people could trade time working for the city as a soldier, scavenger, police, whatever is needed... Marshall creates his own currency with some help from the bank... and people begin a convoy of fuel trucks up from Texas asking for Sanctuary...

The future is uncertain, and starting to get more crowded, by the minute.

Jake Harwell has started to teach classes at the school. They have folks teaching foundry work, and how to run

CNC routers, to how to field dress a deer. Jake Harwell uses the "Gut-less Method" he learned from a local.
It is a good method for field dressing a deer on the move. Which is especially important, once you've got the smell of blood in the air, and eaters on the prowl.

****

"Gut-less Method" of Quartering and for Packing out a Deer/Elk

Every hunter has his or her own preferred method of gutting and or quartering game animals and to be honest there is no right or wrong way as long as meat is properly taken from the field.

1. Lay the deer/elk on its back
2. Then you must cut the penis off the belly of the animal and lay it off to the side to allow urine to drain off.
3. Next, take hold of the back leg and carefully cut just above the anus of the animal along the crease where both legs meet.
4. Working your knife along the pelvic bone work towards the hip socket. Be very careful not to puncture the guts. Once you find the hip socket work your knife into the joint until you hear an audible pop sound. Once you have popped this socket continue working your knife up to the top of the back leg till the leg is completely cut from the body. Repeat steps 3 and 4 for the final back leg.
5. Front shoulders and legs are the easiest pieces of a deer or elk to remove from the carcass. First, take the front should in your hand, then with your knife cut under the armpit.
6. Continue cutting with one hand and pulling with the other. You will notice the front shoulders have no major joints to separate and the removal of the front shoulders is

very quick and easy.

7. Next, you need to roll the carcass on to its stomach to aid in the removal of the back straps. Using the spine of the animal as a reference cutting from the back to the front, cut from the top of the spine down till your knife stops. Using one hand to pull the meat away from the spine, cut and pull down to the base of the neck of the animal. Then, you must go to the back of the animal and then feel for a flat shelf of bone right at the top of the ribs. Once you find this shelf use one hand to pull and the other to cut along this bottom bone shelf to the base of neck of the animal and remove the back strap. Repeat step seven for other backstrap.

8. Finally, pull the hide up to base of the animal's skull, exposing the neck meat for removal. Using the spine again as guide cut along the spine to base of the neck and pull with the other hand to remove the neck meat from the animal.

Chapter 19
Cross the Rubicon

king must be a pauper,
in his heart, if he is to love
his city, he must be a rich man in his
pocket watch, guardian of his time,
care for rich, and poor,
humble/ arrogant,
He sees a mind
not just a body,
for which we'd swoon,
whether ugly's pretty,
or prettys ugly…

The scales of his heart balance
out a spot of snuff on a dress
shirt, every habit, of nodding grace,
a friend who can pick you up, or kick you in the face.
A man you cannot help but like
even in disgrace…

Cocoa, Fl
Jan 15, 2014

It was only after the farm house had been burn up, and slavers captured Torc's old lady that Erin had finally gotten folks interested in her crusade against the Slavers. She also wanted them to consider that it was all rather coincidental that The ones who attacked the house still hadn't found the buildings on the back of the property, and the others felt their camouflaging successful… The damage to the house was extensive which would make defense even more of an issue.

Erin and Mike came over from the Island, as soon as

they heard. In under an hour they were tracking their first group of Slavers, who turned out to be going to some old Sheriff boy's camp… It was bad there. There were piles of dead bodies in various states of decay, and undress. The folks back at the farmhouse were flying reconnaissance, also letting Mike know that… the camp had dogs. They wouldn't be able to just sneak in there without someone knowing… and while the drones had a good weapon system, it wasn't exactly a "precision attack".

He and Erin left and came back the next day with over a 100 men, 20 women. They set up a perimeter, and snipers, and… only the folks in cages came out alive.

Mike has 'em do a thermograph over the entire terrain, so we can map out incoming eaters as well as live wires. Mike and Erin went part of the way, the idea being Mike would lure out as many of them as he could to a "precision sighted location"… Mike would be telling them that he's got an incredible woman for sale. He obviously has c-4 strapped to him, but their curious about this piece of…
"Bam! You disrespect my girl you son of a," Mike says shooting the guy, "What… this woman is a lady! I'll broker no disrespect if I take you to her. He is walking almost all of them out like the pied piper…

After that snipers and everyone else from the side and behind them… They come grind right up into their entire formation from behind. It is ruthless, but it is over quickly. The spare no man, and make sure all of them are dead before checking on the women. Erin goes in first, but "forgets to take off her make-up", you can totally bet that's bull… She loves scaring people.

It is really bad there. There is a pit 30' wide 50' long full of

Dead Man's Kitchen

Eric "Moebius" Morlin

Dead Man's Kitchen

bodies.

The slavers have mutilated some of their captives, often with whatever seemed handy. The also seemed to continue, even after the person they were tormenting had died.
Will had gone to help with medical care, and he was not the first trained person to throw up after what he saw.

After that, Erin doctored herself up like an eater more and more often, telling Mike he could never let her bite him even in play, or she'd hurt him… and she could be a mean biter. Of course, How's that for passive-aggressive… especially considering she knew she is married to a man who loves to be bitten. The good thing in all this, "drive him crazy…" is Really fueled the sex life… but… Erin knows he doesn't accept that she could die tomorrow.
She knows, if she did… She knows.. if he did…
He'd crack.

Chapter 20
EVAC Party of...
(2 months ago)
Cocoa, Fl
Nov. 15 , 2013

Erin went into the other room and called Dr. Reich's cell phone. Erin had went to UCF with Will, before he'd gone off to study Oncology, and she'd decided that she'd rather work in the film industry
pretending to play with blood and guns, and special effects, than live in a lab like her mom, and dad before her...
"Hello," a voice said, there was a lot of background noise.
"Will. Erin here... I had an appointment with..."
"Erin, you and Mike need to get out of town... Things are really bad. I'm talking get out to the farm, and maybe that might not be enough," Will sounds frantic.
"What about you and Cheryl..." Erin says, but Will interrupts, "oh, I'm so... f'ing selfish, I didn't even think about Cheryl..." he pauses," Erin, I'm not sure I'm not dead... I got bit by one of those things, and... I cut my finger off. I spoke with Barry and he
said this thing isn't just here... This is related to all that stuff that's been going on in Africa, and the Middle East, not sure if it is a bioweapon, but it is majorly infectious, and... If I start to tell you they keep moving after their dead... I sound crazy, but... It is happening... I can't be near any of you again until I know what this is... If I'm carrying it... I'll probably have to lock myself away for the next week... ",he pauses on the phone again, "Would you and Mike please grab Cheryl..."
"Oh, course Will, but you need to tell us where you'll be....

Even if it is to swap out iv bags on you while you sleep in a hotel. We don't need to waste time and being exposed cause we're having to track you down... text the info," Erin looks over.

Mike has come into the room. He says, "We'll get Cheryl. Is she at the house?"

Erin repeats, "We'll get Cheryl... Is she at the house?"

"Yes, Will says, "She's at the house, and ... I owe you both..."

"Whatever. Family, "Erin say.

"I know. Family," Will repeats, then says, "My love goes with you all," and hangs up.

<warning intentional spelling errors ahead. Conditions can get turbulent...>

Erin mentioned what Will had said about things dying, and continue to move. Mike made calls and the old neighborhood crew were all going to meet them at a farmhouse on the outskirts of town, near Satellite Blvd. Mike and Erin left an hour later to get everything into their two trucks. A Black Chevy Suburban, and Military Salvage Cougaroan MRAP. Mike was a gun dealer, who mostly dealt in medieval and historical firearms, but... no one could say his Russiaaan built automated machine gun on the vehicle was not historical now... They were all making history...

As they drove across town they saw National Guardsmen, but they knew Mike from back before... when he'd worked for both Dnyyacorp, and later Acadeemi. They should at least be able to get across town without too much trouble. They called Cheryl from the front of her house, and Mike went in to get her... Mike was wearing his glock 19 in the back of his belt, and Kold steel Ink Gladivus... However, Cheryl had already packed her Chevy Charger. The vehicle rumbled when it came to life...

Only Mike noticed how few people came to their windows to look out as they drove by. If fact, they saw no one else until they got to the gas station at the corner of Satellate Blvd.

Satellate Blvd was off a dirt road near the Huffy, a local Gas Station. The front windows of the store were smashed out. There was a Volksvegann beetle (Old School), crashed into one of the gas pumps, and multiple bodies were on the ground. They all appear dead and un moving.

Erin is in the Suburban, and she can see Mike start to slow down... He knew the store owners, but... as Erin starts to take her foot off the gas. She can her Mike starting to engage gears in the MRAP, and they move forward and on...

The house is down a un marked back road. The road forks off several times before they get to the house, each time Erin takes the last fork. When the road dead ends at a large field and a farmhouse.

As they pulled up to the house Mike was thinking about the years he'd spent in the old house. First going to visit with Will, back when he still lived with his parents, and then after a really nasty divorce where, Will got the house, not particularly because either parent cared about Will, but more so they could cheat the other out of the money. The house had become a house for their whole peer group at the time, later, but only after they had been properly vetted would they be joined by girlfriends, who would eventually become... wives.... It was their private place.

The "gang" had all pitched in to help Will keep the house through med school, his internship... They each started a small business on the property to generate "loot" for Will to finish med school. He never faltered, and it didn't hurt that the guys were true to their word. Will always had enough cash for books, classes, etc.

However, Cheryl had to pay for their dates, but she also ran a business on the property, a mini art gallery. and hunting make sure he made it to his classes on time, even arranged a study group for Will, even though, old Congo Billy as they called Bill back at the time… had some weird math phobia. Which meant he could only help Science, and English. Luckily Plush Joseph a weird dj kid from Castleberry was a total Molecular Biology/ Microbiology nerd, as a hobby…

His real business was a nootropics, and exotic foods company… was the perfect tutor for Will all through med school. In a parallel universe

Mike would eventually run his gun restoration business out of a building on the back in of the property. All of them had shops on the property, Bill, Tim, and Torc all had shops of some kind in the same building… Bill ran a garage, focusing on hybrid fuel systems, and fuel alternatives. Torc worked in stained glass, and . Oh, and little Tim had been trying to set up a bar with a tattoo studio in back…

None of it would have been possible if they hadn't worked together, and now they were all starting to come into their "best years.. " the world was going to f*ck all…

Dead Man's Kitchen

Chapter 21
Raiders
Cocoa, Fl
Aug 1, 2014

The night came, and with it came raiders. There were a lot of them, but they didn't realize that Will saw them coming from the house. Will didn't like relying on hi tech over people, but in this instance, it saved them. Bill and the others had built a couple watch tower hidden in the trees, one toward the front of the property, the other toward the back.

Only the raiders were making an obvious feint, and the folks at the farmhouse would have bought it hook line, and sinker. An alarm went off in the South Quadrant of the fence line, and luckily someone looked at the cameras. "F*ck," someone get me a phone, "no I don't want to use the cell." We still don't know their technological capacity, but what we do know is they could intercept cell phone traffic.

"Yeah, Bill, redirect the drone to the woods in the south," Will said. They had charges located out in the marsh, to the west, and outside the gate to the East, and Will blew them now. He also ordered everyone out of the guard towers. They would keep firing with remote weapon systems. The raiders started to lay down fire too. Will could make out hundred from the South though.

The land line started to ring, and Will picked up immediately. "Will, it is bad man, really bad. They must have close to a thousand men. I'm coming back around, but…"

Cha-Doom!

The explosion shook the house.

"Obviously, I ain't going to make it before they breach our walls, and they got a lot of people." Several other explosions soon followed. Will knew one of them was the Hellfire missiles Bill launched. Will knew it would be the first of many. The Raiders had grenade launchers, and hit the house. There were people on it. The raiders outside are hit hard enough to remind them of the "shock and awe" method of combat, unfortunately for them it is on the receiving end.

The raiders who make it in, hit one of the towers with a rocket launcher, and the house as well. When they come back as eaters. They devour their own, but a wild shot hits Jimmy in the forehead, and that's all she wrote. Only a couple of the raiders survive, armed with knives, and Will and the others move in to capture them. They try to fight, but are exhausted. They practically welcome their defeat, as Will and the others kill the hungry who approach them.

Will and others go around and finish the remaining eaters.

Bill is kicking and spitting at the eater who killed Jimmy, and Mike had become odd about not disrespecting the dead, even of the raiders. He killed 'em, but he wouldn't let people beat on 'em and kick on 'em. So… of course he goes up to Bill saying, "You do you a disservice when you disrespect the dead."
"This mother, killed Jimmy," Bill says.
"Nope, that guys gone, and you know it," Mike replies.
"I know your freaked out about your old lady having cancer," Bill starts.
Mike says, "Just, for me. Let the dead flesh be dead."
Bill says nothing else, and after, they've repaired the hole in the wall Mike makes BBQ.

This is his recipe:
****

Mustard base bbq sauce
3 cups of apple cider vinegar
8oz of texas pete
fist full of salt
fist full of fresh cut red pepper
tsp of cayenne pepper boil
Guldens mustard

Eric "Moebius" Morlin

Chapter 22
Morte a Venezia
Venezia, Italy
Aug 3, 2016

It was humid and Piazza San Marco was quiet. Venezia is tricky like that. It is a city which, hides another city underneath it. Do you think anyone tried to build a home so perfectly seamed, as to be airtight, like a ship? That deep down in the much, you might have some domed workshop hidden beneath the deeps; enough air pressure so the water didn't seep in. Ancient Ertuscan cities by the sea, with a basement that goes deep into the deep with their masquerade mask, let others wonder who they are hiding from.

The dead move through the city like a tide, when it grows dark outside the tide comes in, then they disappear with the sun. This isn't to say, they're gone. It is just before dawn as Betrand sits atop one of the old buildings with a bow, and arrow. It is close to dawn, and the eaters numbers have already thinned their numbers. They won't all go off right away, but Bertrand's arm is sore from firing volley after volley, but he had to let off some steam. When the sun comes out a little more he'll go outside and collect his arrows. Some of them got away, but he averages collecting a thousand arrows a night. So, perhaps are returns on a previous investment?

He climbs from the roof of the building he was on, up to to window of the home he shared with Helena. He had in Venezia, over a year, and three months ago. Since then the city had become a home in a way he never thought possible, but he was debating, leaving.

Chapter 23
Rooftop view
Giudecca, Venezia
November 15, 2013

Bertrand arrived from Argentina in Venenzia for work. He is staying in one of the nice hotels in Venezia, not the nicest… modern, in that, what that so many modern hotels are vogue that feels, slightly luxurious, sterile, safe, and like even luxury is a tedious job. He questions if it is true luxury, because of this…

His company has been buying up all the old paper libraries to privatize them. Betrand normally didn't admit this… even to himself, but he knows his employers are thugs like the Medicis, but like the Medicis they are saving the old books, archives, upon archives that must be protected, and the Italian government is no longer up for the task.

Betrand wishes he could save the buildings, himself, but doesn't like to take on those kinds of dreams, because he knows that this way he has the stability of employment, a good wage, pension.

In the afternoon Betrand takes a gondola to Piazza San Marco, which he infers Marco is the name of the island, since the hotel is on Giudecca, and the way the map looks. He'll have to google it later. Afterwards he explores the maze like streets, and ends up in a grotto, or Campi for a while drinking.

Betrand had lived through the economic crash in Argentina and knew what had really happened, how the bankers had robbed the country and blamed it on Peron securing better wages, and it might have worked if Argentina didn't have neighbors, and bankers didn't rob the country, and unions didn't help them by keeping out competition to themselves… The socialists and the capitalists were dividing up the pie, and as usual trying to screw everyone else.

Betrand was 28. He was the youngest of twelve children, and considered a prodigy. He got both babied, and indoctrinated from the time he was three, but from a crazy multicultural tilt. Usually if he tells anyone about how each of his siblings had to tutor him in a language, literature of tongue, the science of that language's people, martial arts of that people, the sciences as viewed by those language.
His father was a professor with doctorates in linguistics, physics, and anthropology, and sometimes Betrand felt… the only person who could understand. He, who was the culmination of a families knowledge.

Helena was America, her father owned an apartment in Venezia, and she had just gotten dump… she'd just broken up with ***hole boyfriend. Who had attempted to break up with her by text. Betrand knows he would have survived without her, but… She had challenged him, changed him even, aber das ist eine Sache für sich…

After walking around through those meandering back streets, Betrand was exhausted. This had been his only day for touristing, he was done, and now, going to check out the "rooftop bar." Usually, such things are disappointingly lame, no decent view, or if the place does have a view there's so much smog and light pollution you can't see it. He was growing, what's the word… erschöpft… um… jaded. It didn't matter in the end. The view was wasted on him once he saw Helena, she looked up, and…

held his gaze. They both held each rapt as he walked up the stairs. Anyone watching would have thought she'd been waiting for him. She stood up and he looked behind him, just to make sure there wasn't someone else...

She said in perfect Italian, "Il suo nome non è Iain è vero?" She asked him.

"No, Ho quasi , vorrei che fosse," He replied.

"Non è un jerkface," Helena said, "il est juste que vous pourriez être son jumeau, and that is probably the extent of my Italian. Scusami, I'm sorry..."

"Sorry, because I'm the twin of a jerkface?" Betrand asks. And then the young woman laughs again, covering her mouth, "I did just say that didn't I."

"You're American?" Betrand asks as if, no worries it all makes sense now, "I thought you were native."

"I'm good with accents," Helena replies, "So, where are you from? Or.. are you from Venezia, you have a similar accent."

"Nope, I'm a doppleganger, too." He says.

"What?" Helena asks.

Bertrand chuckles, "Literally, it is supposed to be like your double, but I just mean you've got a good ear for languages..."

Helena laughs, it is uber nerdy and totally cute at the same time. He has rarely felt like he wanted to remember someone's laughter again. At least not since he'd traveled right after college, man his dad was pissed, Mr. I don't push you about anything, had, had plans that Bertrand had decided to take a break from... that was the job he took, his vacation from his family with oppressively high standards. He finds himself smiling back at this girl he just met and says, "I'm Bertrand. Please to meet you."

"Helena," she says, "and you're from Dopplegangia?"

Betrand breaks out in a genuine laugh of his own. He didn't know when the last time that happened, and says, "Oh, sorry about that... I'm bad about taking things off

Eric "Moebius" Morlin

track, and seeing connections no one else seems to… I'm from Argentina."

"Oh, wow! I love it there, your country is so beautiful. Do you salsa?" Helena asks.

Bertrand says, "Sadly, I do not…."

"Well then," Helena says sweeping the air with her hand, as for one second she pretends to turn away disinterested, but then she's back, locking eyes with him, and says, "So what brings you to Venice…"

"I'm here exploring old libraries for work, um," Betrand says, "Were you waiting for someone?"

"Oh, that, there was this guy I met back when I worked for Cirus des Dragons, named Iain, and I agreed to meet him for a drink," Helena answers.

"I just," he starts to say, "were you guys close? I just wouldn't want to interrupt the jerkface, and your dinner plans…"

Helena laughs again, interrupting, "no, we tried to date, but my Italian really isn't all that great."

Betrand thinks, "thank you God, Let's get out of here before jerkface shows up." Instead he says, "I know you Americans looks don't on it, but would you care to step outside with me for a minute so I can have a cigarette."

"Only one condition," She says coyly.

"You smoke too?" He asks, she nods, and they are off into the night air…

Chapter 24
Always that one Dirty Bastard
central Florida
Aug 15, 2014

He had a campfire going. He put the dutch oven in the fire, then flipped the lid. Mike threw coals in on top. He and Erin were sleeping in the woods near Sanford. She was dressed like and Eater, and was chained to the bed. Mike was wearing explosives rigged to explode if his heart stopped, or he flipped a dead man's switch.
It was his response to Erin wanting to dress up like a Eater half the time. They were on the way back out to the city in the trees, as they called it amongst themselves...
Only something was wrong, there was a fire. Before they got to the camp, Mike heard a clicking. Which he knew to be a warning outsiders were in the surrounding woods and to meet somewhere else. It also warned of eaters.
Mike pushed some dirt over the fire, and then cut Erin's rope and disappeared into the woods. Erin watches the surrounding forest for moment, and slowly she backs into the darkness.

Mike encounters a lone raider, looking harried, like he's sure he's being pursued. Mike takes out his krimbit. He stalks the other soldier, moving to intercept him, as he does he slices the tendons on the inside of both the man's arms, then covers his mouth, and explains if he didn't want killed he'll answer questions, he doesn't seem inclined to cooperate and even tries to work the weapon with his working fingers. Mike smashes the guy in the face with the

Dead Man's Kitchen

Eric "Moebius" Morlin

stock of his gun. He doesn't know why he doesn't kill him, then he disappears back into the forest.
"If my girls are hurt," Mike whispers as he goes off into the woods. He circles back behind the raider, and attacks from the opposite direction from where he left. It is probably disconcerting, and worse when he cuts the guys Achilles.

Mike then leaves to meet the survivors, at their supply drop. Only he stops just before he gets there to enter what looks to be a deadfall, and is actually a shed made to look like a deadfall. Inside is the back up for the computers running their camera system. It allows him to looks at the surrounding area, and see bodies everywhere. Eaters feasted like ghouls. He sees men leaving to the South west. He also sees the folks from their camp at the drop, as he scans the area. It looks like almost everybody. Who… someone was missing.

Mike goes to meet them. In front is Krista, she looked like she was much older, but held herself straighter. Mike asks the question, "Misty and Cat. Where? Who's not here," Mike asks, "Dead or captured?" "More important things Mike. You always tell us to keep you focused in situations like this, unless you're brain storming. We were able to blow a bunch of our booby traps, and escape to the South. It was some of the ranchers men. Harris, was leading 'em. Him, and Mowley, looks like he sold us out to the raiders. I don't think the rancher is in on it, but hard to tell. The left toward the South West,"

Krista tells Mike, "Misty, Cat, Anna, and Brigitte. You don't understand how many of them there were Mike. They practically had an army, hundreds if not thousands. How could they have organized like that Mike? They had tanks, and rocket launcher thingies. The mines took out a few, but we had to take out those tanks. Misty said, if we didn't we'd be facing them again… We didn't have a lot of time, but… that much we agreed on, and we drew straws. I'm sorry." Krista is silent. "Sorry for what," Mike says, "Looks like you saved everyone." "Not everyone," Krista say, and starts crying, "and we lost our homes. Everything."

"Are you crazy hon? You all just saved each other from a major assault. You didn't even need me, and were able to hold your own… All I'm saying is y'all are more important to me than a place I am living. Y'all are my family. You all saved my family, but saving each other. Misty, Anna, Cat and Brigette are our first national heroes. Be ye not afraid," Mike says, "You've done the hard work. Now, did we get all of them?"

"The Ranchers men, looked to have got away. His other men were starting to turn. We got out," Krista says. She's still crying. "Yes, you survived, and we're gonna follow them back to where they came from," Mike says.

They all nod in agreement.

Later Mike goes back to recover the venison. This is how he prepared it.

This is the recipe he used for his Venison.

****

Venison

You'll need:
A Dutch Oven
Venison.
1 carrot
1 onion
1-2 potatoes,
1 tsp salt,
1 tsp ground black pepper
1 tbsp rosemary

Optional:
aYou can marinade the Vennison ahead of time
by soaking it in a mixture of:
red wine with:
1 tsp. Gulden's Mustard
1 tbsp Worcestershire sauce.
1/3 cup red wine
¼ cup olive oil
1 tbsp brown sugar
1 tbsp soy sauce
2 cloves fresh garlic

D**irections**:
The ideal here, is to cook slow at low temperature with carrots, onions, potatoes, season with salt, rosemary, and pepper. You set up a fire, and later in the evening you put your dutch oven in the fire pit, flip the lid, and fill it with hot coals, so it cooks all the way through. Take your time.

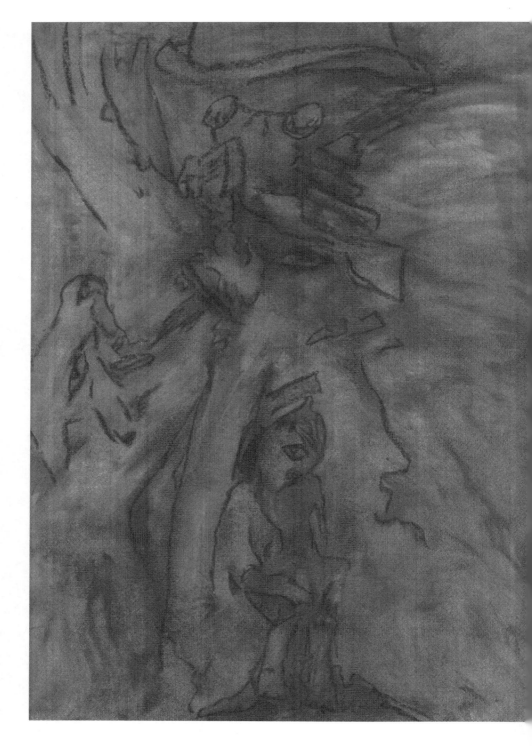

Chapter 25
No one to name the Storms

Charleston, SC
August 18, 2014

Juan hadn't gone back to work, that night. Instead he had dumped the body, and driven North, as if he could escape the coming carnage and ended up in Charleston. The city was in Chaos when he arrived. He didn't know why at the time, but he'd driven right up to the gate of the local Naval base. The base commander had been sporadically letting people through the gate if they could show they had a useful skill set. All others were eventually being given the boot. Which had resulted in some rather dramatic displays of people's discontent, including more than one suicide by gate guards.

After the first month the gates were closed to all outside personnel. So Juan had made it just by the skin of his teeth. He was given a job in the base print shop. Juan had worked in printing for almost 2 decades before he decided that he'd rather handle dead bodies, and now it was his only means of escape. He had considered suicide momentarily, but only just.

The print shop on base only needed him one or two days a week to put out the base newsletter. The rest of the time he was what was called a floater. This is to say he took what jobs were available, and needed folks to work them.

Occasionally that job was to scavenge for the military, looking for supplies. Occasionally they ran into families, who needed the supplies more, and Juan would throw a box of MREs to 'em when no one was looking. Once or twice he'd encountered children running wild, they stared from the distance, but never came any closer…

A lot of time had passed, but now a storm had been sitting off the coast building for days. It had hit Cuba, 3 days ago. Those who had access to short wave radio received broadcasts that Cuba had weathered the storm. What they radio didn't say was, Cuba had dealt with their eaters. They'd killed anyone who got sick as soon as it started. It was one of a few scattered countries that had managed to stay relatively stable. People tried to come in by boat from the states, sometimes they were taken in…
Usually they were turned away.
Charleston was fractured, even before the storm hit. There was still power at the Naval Base, and near what had once been 841st Trans Battalion. There was no one to name the storm when it hit Sullivan Island. Katrina in 2005 had only been a Category 3.

This new storm was a category 5 with sustained winds over 160 mph. Sullivan's island was stripped clear, as if humans had never been to the Americas. The streets are at least temporarily clear of Eaters, perhaps they'd been blown away like debris. The flooding is extensive, and the areas surrounding the Naval Complex had stabilized, but with the coming of the storm flooding took out much of the cities French Quarter. John Islands had stabilized their power grid, but pulled off line during the storm.

The base commander has discussed opening the gates to some civilian traffic again, for trading and such, but there has been a lot of disagreement about whether this is wise.

Chapter 26
How to maintain

Cocoa, Fl
August 20, 2014

The farmhouse wasn't rebuilt after the fire, although Will and the others have worked to expand their defenses. The slavers who were caught were questioned politely, and shot. Will was against torturing them, instead had those that "got away" followed back to their base, with a new drone system the guys developed... In that time they discovered what they thought the main camp, was only one of a great many. The one outside Orlando was more like a dozen of the other camps put together... This wasn't something that would just go away. They had tens if not hundreds of thousands of people, not including the enslaved.

However, thanks to the help of some folks down at the port, and the now defunct air force base. They had missile systems, and people to operate it. (at least until the tech failed). However, Will knew that waiting for a force with those kinds of numbers was a losing proposition. It looked to him like the raiders were planning on using the same method of the great Mongol leader Genghis Khan.

This is to say the leader of the raiders planned to use the loved ones of their enemies in the front lines, as a Khan had... Partially as a distraction... forcing them to fight their own, or to protect those they love, or... kill them themselves... if they weren't killed by them. All the while bringing in more and more warriors.

In the end, they would make a dance floor over their enemies, and dance upon the bodies of their enemies until they had broken all their bones… It is said by some this is why the Russians act the way they do with outsiders…

Dead Man's Kitchen

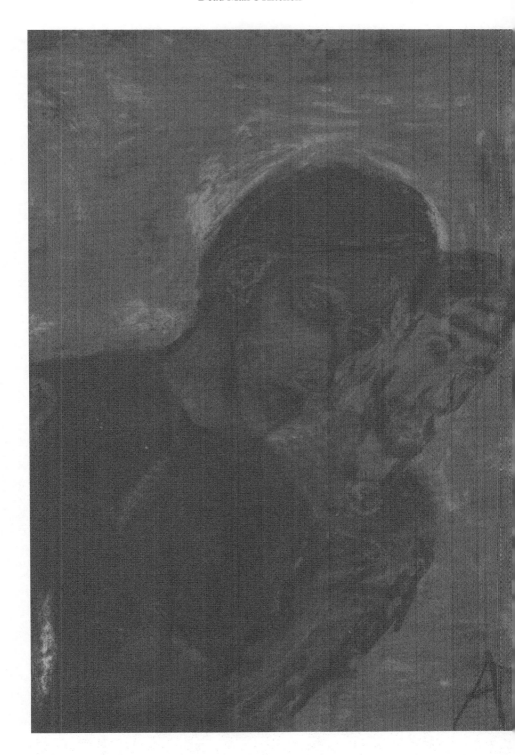

Will is talking to Mike and Erin on the front porch of the farmhouse. After the outer walls were breached, the men had to decide not just on repairs, but how to prevent things from going this way next time.

The turn of the century Florida farmhouse could be reinforced and up graded, but it would require a lot of steel, concrete, and lexan for the windows.

Cheryl walks out onto the porch, bringing everyone their latest round of lemonade. Will had a folder next to him, containing Erin's fMRI scans.

There was now a full hospital on the property, using tractor trailers with their own power, and everything a young doctor could dream of working with including electron microscope, fMRI, you name it… Again, this would only work as long as they were able to scavenge the technology to maintain it. Will's hope was that they had saved enough of the medical equipment that, it might be possible to keep going by partsing out other machines as they went, that while the technological level society had been at before the plague was going to be difficult to maintain. They might be able to use what they had as a stop gap method until such time as they could reinvent the technology again.

This would be far harder if they didn't start doing something now, without air conditioning, or dehumidifiers the technology would not be easy to maintain and if their population has been drastically depleted it could easily drop the country, or even the world into another dark ages, one from which they would not easily recover.

Humanity was on a precipice, and looking down he could always picture the hungry horde below them.

Eric "Moebius" Morlin

Which got Will to thinking, about how little they knew of what was happening in the rest of the world…

However, he didn't let his worries ruin the good news…

"I don't know how, what to say, Erin," Will said, "Your cancer has gone into total remission…"

"Now if only the world would get better," Erin said, but she lit up with a smile, and then followed with, "I still feel Incredible."

"Yeah, you do," Mike interjects, " but I also have something I need to bring up. Except, and I don't know if I am bringing this up to you as a doctor or friend, but… back where we're living… Erin has attacked a few folks," Mike says.

Will chuckles, then when he sees Mike looks serious, Erin abashed he says, "Okay, so what's all this then… I don't see any bite marks on you."

"I am able to fight her off. Only, she bit one of… she bit a young girl who was pursuant. A girl, she'd been trying to get to…" Mike makes air quotes, as he says," take care of me, when she was gone… but then one day… She shows up all zombied out, in special f/x make up, and goes after her. Luckily, Donna was around she was able to trap Erin and… She had bitten the girl's ear. Tore it pretty badly actually…

Most of the others have managed to avoid injury."

Will looks at Erin who shrugs, and he's like," Well, you know I'm not a shrink, and I can ask you all sorts of stuff, like Do you feel more in control, when you…"Only Erin interrupts.

"I don't feel like anyone is in control when I…"Erin replies.

"How about when you're with Mike? And you're pretending to be feral," Will asks.

"I feel totally in control," Erin says, "it's like you've got this feedback loop coming directly from people's... You can feel people's fear."
"She's proactively hunting down, and knocking out the competition," Will says.
"Darn it Will, you rat!"
"I figured that, but... I'm not interested in anyone else," Mike says.
"Don't tell me," Will says, "tell her..."
Mike looks over to Erin, and she growls at him, Feral...

"I love you hon, and I'm not really interested in anyone else..." Mike says.
"Not really interested in anyone else," Erin says," You hear this Jerkface..."
"What do you want me to say, that I don't even notice these other women, only it would be cruel to let them know they aren't even a shadow of a reflection of you," Mike says," or how I must struggle to conceal my joy when I am with you, lest you see I feel like I have already walked into heaven when you stand by my side, and..."
Erin groans," laying it on pretty thick," Erin replies, "there Shakespeare."
"I will lay thee down on the thickest fullest of downy beds, my lady, but get over letting this raging beast take thee..."
"enough hon," Erin says.

Dead Man's Kitchen

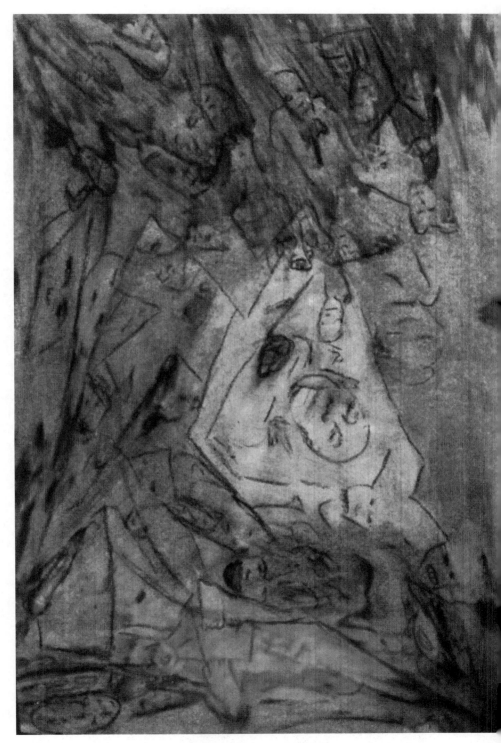

"I just want you to get it. I don't want anyone else... sure I'm easy, but don't leave me alone with other women, "Mike says.
"I will gut you. If you think about sullying my bed with another woman..."Erin starts.
"So, you like feeding her jealousy, and what the fuck kinda drama are y'all up to? This is a crazy time to be doing crazy stuff, that could get one or both of you killed..."Will says.
"Yes, dad," they both reply.
"ungrateful," Will pretends to storm off...

Will was supposed to be holding a war council tonight, but he figured they could take a night off as long as he had folks monitoring with drones. The enemy was large. They had sheer numbers with which they could overrun them. This was ignoring the fact that they could field their victims, and use them for fodder, as well field an army, and one mobile enough they should probably consider relocating rather than attempt to hold off against future raids. The drones were up almost 24/7 now. They had active thermal overlays, but more important they were able to acquire access to the old military satellites thanks to some help from folks hold up at Cape Canaveral.

In the kitchen,
Will made Sour Cream to go with a baked potatoes. If you don't know how to make Sour Cream, you'll need to look at the recipe below.

Ingredients:
½ cut milk
1 ½ teaspoon distilled white vinegar
2 cups heavy cream

Mix milk and vinegar together. Afterwards pour the cream in and cover the container. Let chill for 24 hours.

CHAPTER 27
Dead, Dead, Dead
CENTRAL FLORIDA
August 21, 2014

The slaver camp is to the Southeast of Orlando. It is subdivided into sections. The captured are kept in heavy metal cages. The place smells of rotting bodies, and human waste. There is a group of Yurts toward the middle of camp, surrounded by a group of armed women.

In the Yurt toward the center of camp, a man sits on a throne. His name is Brock Warren. He was a roofer before the outbreak. A group of men stand to either side of him, and two kneel on the ground. The ones on the ground are raiders who led the assault on the compound. They had directed the attack from behind, and in doing so guaranteed the survival.

"So, let's summarized", the man on the throne says, "You took 800 men with tanks, rocket launchers, and one of my tanks… and you're the only guys who survived?"
"About two dozen of us surviv," one of the men had started to reply, when Brock interrupts, "I heard what you told me the first time. Did I feel I didn't get the gist of things? You led my people to their death."
"I didn't," the man says, and Bang. Brock shoots him in the forehead.

Brock turns toward the other man, who remains quiet, "and you are okay with me just shooting you? Yet you weren't on the front lines leading my men… a contradiction."

"I serve you until my death," Horace answers, "just like I told you I would. However, you had me under the command of another, and while it might have served you if I had killed him once I realized his incompetence. It wasn't my place. I await your next orders."

Brock nods his head, knowing it consistent with the man he's seen.
"You will prepare an assault force of 2000 men, with another couple thousand slaves to stand in front of 'em. You will have Stinger and Patriot Missiles. You will destroy them, and bring me their heads," Brock says.
"By your leave, my liege," Horace says.

****

August 25, 2014

In the days that follow Horace, asks for several men that he has known during other operations. Horace wants to send in a reconnaissance force of 12 men. They had all previously served in the military except for Issacs.

The problem is, that when they arrive. The farmhouse has already been destroyed. There are bodies everywhere, and eaters have begun to fill in the gaps. The who compound is completely stripped. It looks like the ranchers might be involved. Horace's people were able to identify the bodies of some of the dead by their clothing.

"Those treacherous hillbillies, " Brock rages, "I want you to go in there and skin those prick."
"Yes, sir," Horace says.

The ranchers had their own people out in the woods,

and saw a reconnaissance force coming in. He recognized them as Brock's men immediately. The scout disappears into the woods immediately. Burgance signals Rebecca to call the other families, Cheryl would wake the boys, Molly would start making breakfast.

If you asked Burgance why they did it, he'd say because they're thieving slavers. He trusted them only to try and betray him, or they could have found out he was skimming on them in some of their transactions. Whatever the case, there were too many of them. Burgance doesn't have many men, but he does have cattle.

The Ranchers are able to get their families out the back of the farm with a majority of the men. Burgance will greet them, and while they do that, he'd have somebody drive his cattle right up their ass.

His greeting is several .30 caliber machine guns, and the cattle had just started charging successfully into soldiers when they heard the tanks. That's plural. The cows were stampeded just as Burgance got shot through the left orbital, and went out the back of his skull. His other eye spasmed as we watched the cattle charge by him..

They were firing on the cattle with machine guns. Burgance loved his animals. He also knew that unless he survived none of those beef carcasses would be salvaged.

Those lives given, only to let their sacrifice fall to the wayside. It was just such a wretched waste. All that food would go to waste because of those morons. He tried to get up, but his legs failed him, and he slid around in his own blood, and then silence.

Far too many of the Rancher people escaped for Horace's liking, but being able to skin Burgance and a few of his higher ups meant he wouldn't have to go back to Brock with another failure. They had capture a few of the women, children, and a few older farm hands… As he was sure Brock would want someone to continue running the farm. Horace silently wished that would be him, but knew he would be granted no such solace. He was to be a killer and nothing more.

CHAPTER 28
Drawn and Quartered
New Orleans, LA
August 24, 2014

A group of Train kids are sitting across from the old Mint, in a parking lot next to what was once a Chinese restaurant. They are doing lines of Crystal Meth as they talk casually. Occasionally a group of eaters come close and the young men take a break from their festivities to dispatch them with machetes.

The entrance to the Marigny was blocked off when a Tractor Trailer drove into a building. The Quarter remains overrun with eaters, but mostly they stay inside during the day. The city has large swathes of territory where it is still considered unsafe to travel. City park, and some of the other graveyards for one. The older eaters who hadn't turned to mush after being exposed to the humidity, haven't fallen apart like people thought they would. While hhere are always a few random eaters out during the day, most people joke about them being vampires. This only becomes a problem when folks start to believe it, and get overly cocky, overly noisy, and then they find themselves overrun, outnumbered, and dead.

After the attack, Liam and the others relocated to an abandoned children's hospital, located elsewhere in the city. The problem was making it look like it was still vacant, and setting up some medieval style booby traps for those foolish enough to wander in.

Liam also started a rooftop. He built up the roof with plastic tarps and pallets, so he could try to keep the rain from settling up top, and eventually bringing down the roof on top of them. They brought in bags of fertilizer from a local hardware store, for some reason no one had touched the place and Liam made good use of it. They got every bag of fertilizer, seeds, plastic tubs and pots to grow in, generators, the place was like paradise.

They took the fertilizer by truck to a abandoned lot near the kid's hospital, and were able to get everything in by wagon.
On the lower floors Ken took out stairways, and floors, so folks coming in to strip out copper wire and such would think the whole place had been worked over. Occasionally there would be a cabinet situated at just the right place to climb up through a hole in the ceiling above.
Nobody noticed Ken had got the elevator running, unless they were in the building when they ran it. They had killed the bell for the doors, and the lights in it. So it wouldn't easily give them away, and the generator powering it, sat several floors up, and no one could hear it purring. Along.

Liam and the others traded with several groups throughout the city. One group recycles everyone's metal with a foundry they built and so they trade for scrap metal. Easy enough considering how many abandoned cars there are. They trade parts, homemade guns, and reloaded brass for food, fuel, and other necessities. They also make plows, threshers, hoes, metal gates for folks who want to replace the one they had previously with something... sturdy.
A hundred pounds of metal will get you a couple guns, some tools, couple cases of shells. Essentially, about 10-20% of what you gave them. If you're trading food, especially processed food you can get a much better deal, as

people are coming to realize that unless they have dents, or are swollen, most can food will last decades. It won't always taste good, but it won't kill you. The metal guys have gotten pretty skillful over the last year.

Charity hospital wasn't possible to salvage, although groups have gone in to recover bandages, medicines, dope, etc. Some groups come back, some are never seen from again. However, when they do make it out, usually they are working for a group that has taken over one of the bigger hotels and turned it into a fortress. They call themselves Knights Hosptiallers. They will trade or pay for supplies they feel they need, but mostly seem to operate on donations. If someone is sick they can go there and get treated for free.
Supposedly a lot of the folks working there were attending med school at UNO before the Eaters came.

After the raid on the house, Liam and the others are far more careful about who they let see them come and go, and who could come home with them.

A lot of the hotels were designed back when the French, or Spanish controlled the city, and so have huge courtyards that could be used for parking, or what not, and make the buildings similar in design to an old castle. The parking lots often are now being used to cultivate. Ken has found such a property which he has camouflaged as a huge garbage dump. He also set up bamboo wind chimes, not so much because he has become a closet hippie, but because he doesn't want folks to be able to hear what he's up to.
In the main courtyard of the house he "maintains", he has started raising animals. He has a duck pond, turkeys,

goats, chickens, geese, turkeys, a cow and bull, and so far no one is the wiser. The manure is great fertilizer, and he's been growing potatoes and other root crops to assist with that. He prepares other "shit piles" to dehydrate and cook manure and even human feces in a couple locations, in the hopes it will become a revenue stream on its own.

If you asked him he'd tell you he is using the Norfolk method of crop rotation. It cycles through beans/legumes, wheat, root crops, then barley. It is supposed to keep the soil healthy and full of nutrients. Ken also uses a wood chipper to grind up the bones of corpses for Phosphate, and ask for potassium.

Whatever the case his animals seem fat and happy.

Chapter 29
Alligator soup
Gainesville, Fl
August 25, 2014

Mike is down on a wooden pier watching Erin go swimming. No f/x make up today. If you were to look at their vehicles you'd think them a military convoy, MRaps, and trucks with tanks on the back. Erin is swimming with two younger girls they met, barely 14 named Destiny and Charity. They've been surviving on their own for over a year. Will sees no problem adding them to the parade, but when the two young girls reveal they know where a gas truck is... It is like they become designate warrior princesses.

Erin wants Mike to adopt them, and he says he doesn't see anything wrong with that, if the girls are okay with it. "They used to have a momma and a poppa, and," Mike starts, then, "just make sure they're okay with it…"

They had been worried if they'd have enough fuel to last them through the winter, but between the fuel truck, and other sources they find along the way… with Florida being thankfully warmer than it is up North, Will said they should be good for some time, but they should probably look to a way to get fuel.

They had been slowly working their way north, using drones to scout ahead, and avoiding settlements that seemed well established. Occasionally they spoke with locals, and discovered the slavers had attempted to come this way the previous summer, but had been kept at bay by an alliance between Ocala, Gainesville, and some of the smaller North Florida cities.

Occasionally their calvacade would find places that were just dead. No eaters, no living folks, nothing… They stripped everything from these places like locusts with wire strippers. In a couple of places they found lumber supply warehouses, or grocery store distribution centers. Ironic, if the locals had just known this was there, they might have been able to last awhile longer.

All the things to sustain them for months if not years to come.

Now, everyone is taking a break. Will and the others are resting. He, Mike, and Erin had hung around long enough to see if the raiders had bought it. Burgance and the ranchers had set Mike up, and cost the lives of Misty, Cat, and the others. Mike had in turn framed them for taking out the farmhouse.

Mike let the ranchers he knew, weren't involved with the attack, escape with their families. A few of them he hunted down personally in the dead of night, and used them to feed the alligators. It wasn't so much because they'd killed people he cared for, as that they had gotten near Erin.

However, when he saw what the raiders did to Burgance a day later, Mike found himself reconsidering his stance. However, Mike also knows they need to watch those raiders and plan out some way to quarantine them, if not just slaughter them outright, even if it means killing them with all their hostages. He knew the raiders would show them no mercy.

CHAPTER 30
INTERMISSION

It will be hypothesized by the generations that follow that those who were called Eaters, were not actually dead, in the traditional sense, but rather the midbrain had been actually been hi-jacked by a biological organism. Which tried to operate its host as if it were a cold blooded animal, or reptile.

It is claimed that this did not actually kill the host, but rather put it in a kind of stasis, however, over time certain tissues such as the brain and other internal organs were not designed to operate at these temperatures, and so there was a gradual deterioration of function, until eventual collapse.

However, this biological agent has yet to be identified.

There are other theories, some more esoteric than others, involving demons, possession, alien parasites, a gate way to other dimensions, Gene spicing, GMOS, biological weapons, mass poisoning, and the list goes on. As there has been no definitive proof of any, or all of these. They are marked down to pure conjecture until such time as it can be proven otherwise.

Part II
Where the Dead find Rest

Chapter 31
<u>Beyond Dreams</u>

Wayne wakes to the light of the sun in his eyes. He covers his eyes to sit up, reaching into his jacket pocket to recover a pack of cigarettes. He lights his cigarette, and draws in a breath just as he looks out over the horizon to see bodies everywhere. He starts to cough, hacking up smoke and phlegm. He finds himself choking, as he tried to clear his throat to breathe. He leans over the side of the tarp he had been sleeping on to throw up, only to notice the very ground around him is composed of corpses.

Wayne had thought he'd gone camping, and that was why he was sleeping outside, but he remembers this is not his last memory. It is an older memory, and the mountain top he'd camped on is long gone. Now there are only corpses as far as the eye can see. He knows his sense of smell is impaired from years of smoking, but recognizes that he should smell something. There are no flies in the air, no stench of decay.

Wayne considers the drug use of his youth, and how perhaps this is merely some flashback of drugs awoken in his body by… Only the more he looks around at the faces of the people lying cold around him. They look as if they had all come to one place to sleep. Occasionally he will see someone marred with injury, but most of the bodies have few visible blemishes, no sign of decay.

"This isn't possible," he says out loud, and then is startled by the utter silence around him. He'd thought if he had asserted that this was not reality, then reality might come rushing back in, but nothing happens. He feels certain that he has gone deeply, and utterly insane. Wayne starts to stand, and feels the ground beneath him shift, and in a few moments he is running as an avalanche of bodies beneath him falls away to the distant valley floor.

It is in that moment he finds himself thinking, "Ye though I walk through the Valley of Death. I shall fear no evil."
He doesn't remember the rest of the passage. Wayne notices now he is standing on a man's face. There is no where he can stand without being in someone's face, or their ass, or their..
There is no ground.
None.
The people who lay on the ground around him all appear dressed, and he can see backpacks, and grocery bags, and… after searching for a moment he comes to realize that there is food in the grocery bags. It looks untouched. The bananas in one bag are still a bright yellow.

How the F*ck can this be happening?

Wayne is hungry, and so he starts eating banana, a jar containing beets, some fried chicken. He wolfs it down as if he hasn't eaten in years, but finds he cannot help but watch the wilderness around him, under his weight. He sees a woman that looks familiar and ends up digging through her pockets to discover she had lived in his home town. All the bodies in his vicinity are from his home town. One body he recognizes as a kid that was in the news. He'd been murdered, and no one had ever identified the killer. The kid is holding the identification card, of another man Wayne had seen around town and he can't help but wonder.
There is death as far as the eye can see, no movement, no trees, no rivers. For a moment Wayne considers that

this is Hell. He wasn't exactly a good guy. He never went to church on Sundays, partied too much, prayed a good bit, but it was mostly for God to help him get his shit together, and God never actually spoke with him. He found himself closing his eyes, and praying. He felt stupid when he opened his eyes, back where he started, vacant eyes staring up at him.

Then Wayne gets a really crazy idea, as he starts digging through the bodies, pushing those he has dug through previously over the cliff side. Occasionally he'll find something he deems useful, which he sets to one side. Only then, he finds her…

Leigh. She had died just before the boy. They'd gone to school together. He used to take her to the park. She was pale, lifeless, but it was her. Wayne carried her back out of where he'd been digging, throwing more bodies over the side as he went. He doesn't have his tarp anymore. It went over with the collapse, but he scavenges around until he finds another. It isn't a tarp, it's a bed sheet, and he lays it out and puts her on top.

Wayne starts to talk to her corpse. "You don't understand," he said, "I loved you so much… I love you. Only you died, and I had a break down. I dropped out of school for almost a year. You remember how I was."

She says nothing. There is no rise and fall of breath, no fluttering of eye lashes, no pulse. Wayne finds himself sobbing. Eventually he makes a travois, with which he can drag her and what food he decided upon behind him.

In looking from on top of corpse mountain, as Wayne would dub it, he could see bodies as far as the eye could see.

Except to the left of where the sun rose, what would be North if they were still on Earth. East is always to the right of North. In that direction, the sky seems darker, as if there might be a storm in the distance. The ground there might be covered in bodies as well, but he can't tell.

Wayne talks to Leigh's corpse constantly, and is precisely what he is doing a woman walks up on his camp.
"I thought I heard someone," the woman says. She is attractive, and has long auburn hair. She is dressing in a orange jumpsuit, and has lots of brightly colored bits of cloth tied to her in places
" Well, thank goodness," she says, "for a minute there, I thought I was going crazy."

The woman falls silent, and then starts laughing. At first Wayne stares at her, but now she seems to laugh at his stoicism as well, and finally he can't help but laugh with her. Finally, the both stop laughing and the woman points at Leigh, and says, "Friend of yours."

Wayne nods.
"She... We used to go out when I was growing up, and," Wayne goes silent again, shrugging his shoulders, "I just wanted her back."

"I'll bet," the woman says.
"It ain't nothing perverted," Wayne says.
"No one says it was," the woman replies, "My name is Kaitlin. I've been here going on a month now..."
"A month," Wayne looks up, "Where the.. Where the Hell are we?" he asks her.

"No clue, but I met a guy who claimed that if we went that way," Kaitlin says, pointing the same direction Wayne had been traveling, "supposedly we'll find answers."

Wayne nods.
The two of them sit and eat in silence.
"Huh. It's kinda funny that we can sit and talk to dead people for hours, but once we meet up with someone… all the insecurities come right back out."
Wayne just nods again, and says nothing for a while. Finally he says, "uh, you can travel with us if you want."
"Us? Oh," Kaitlin replies, then, "sure."

When they sleep at night, Wayne sets up a bed that is big enough for all three of them. He doesn't discuss this with the other woman. He just makes the bed, covers up Leigh's corpse with blankets, then sets his own bedding up beside her, leaving a space for Kaitlin should she decide to curl us as well. The living girl and the dead woman like two bookends. Wayne cries in his sleep. Which causes Kaitlin to wake up sometime during the night. She speaks to him in a soothing voice, brushing his hair from his face. She thinks he is handsome for being so F'ing crazy. She knows this is the proverbial pot calling the kettle black, and chuckles softly to herself.

She doesn't want to fall in love with a man who is dragging the corpse of his ex-lover around, she went through that, at least figuratively in her last life, or what she can remember of it. Only, she finds herself laying there smelling the odor of his body, a musk that dominates any of the other smells in the air, and nuzzles up next to Wayne and goes to sleep.

No one can complain they don't eat well in the days that

follow. After several days of taking sponge baths, and sleeping next to each other… their clothing starts to become well ripe, and so they have to search through some of the surrounding bodies for clean clothing.

Kaitlin strips several people So she can get long johns, a hooded heavy coat, and some other things. Wayne strips an old hunter of some Goretex hunting gear, but Kaitlin also has him take several other outfits. Wayne also finds a tent, though neither is sure they want to consider nailing down tent pegs in the cleft of someone's innards.

Wayne can't help but steal glances at the full figured woman stripping naked next to him. Whereas, she watches him full on, half smiling to herself. She knows it won't be long before she breaks him down.

A few nights later, they are all three laying together, when she asks him something in a near whisper, so he has to turn around to speak with him.
"what?" he asks.
"I said, tell me a story," she says, and Wayne finds himself laughing.
"and hold me closer, it is really cold out," She tells him.
As they start to drift to sleep, Kaitlin rolls over, pressing her ample bottom against Wayne. She can already feel his hard on, as he starts snoring. The young woman feels a rage of hormones, like being in a place full of dead people is the antithesis of having a vagina. She finds herself removing her top layer of pants, so it is just a pair of long johns between her and the sleeper. She undoes the Mudd flap in the back of the long johns, and rubs up against him. She has never felt less in control, and is tempted to just unzip and ease him inside her… but recognizes that she

wouldn't want this done to her, and stops herself. In the early morning, she can feel the boy pushing and grinding against her. She reaches back to unzip his pants, and pushing his underwear to the side. He gasps, but after a few moments she can hear the subtle sounds of him breathing deeply in sleep.

Long into the morning they grind against each other in the half fog of sleep. Wayne has hooked his fingers into the cleft of her pelvis, pulling her ass to him. Kaitlin grabs at his ass trying to pull him into her, when finally she decides to just guide his cock between her legs. She can feel so close to being inside her…

"What?!" she hears Wayne say, "I can't be doing this… I thought you were," and he starts to turn away, but Kaitlin is having none of it.

She holds on to his ass, gyrating against him, this time guiding him with her other hand, and he gives. She feels as Wayne pushes his penis up inside her. She gasps. She doesn't even remember the last time she had sex, much less with a stranger, although, she knows this isn't accurate as he slowly rhythmically pushes into her, and she tries to guide him to that place inside, where all the noise, and the everything will be pushed aside. She cries out.

Wayne lifts himself into a kneeling position behind her, propping her ass in the air, this time drawing back as if he is thinking about pulling away, only to thrust deep into her. He's teasing her, as one of his hands comes around to rub against her clit, and she starts to cry out.

"Yes, take it," She says. Her hand reaches back to cup his scrotum in one hand, and she starts to work to milk him, milk his essence into her. She can feel is cum inside her, as his cock throbs, bouncing up and down. He pulls ass tight against him, and then goes to lay down back beside her.

He hasn't pulled out, instead she feels the warmth of his cock, the ice cold of his cum, and the fall to sleep.

AFTERWARD:

It feels like it has been years since I last put out a book... (it has). This book was a long, long time in the making, but... hopefully it has been worth the wait.
I would like to thank some folks for help on the book:

Niall Jackson for his translation of Glaswegan vernacular, and dialogue translations.
I am not much of a football guy, or as the Americans call it, Soccer, but... when I was homeless reciting poetry, and traveling I met some cool guys in Glasgow. Afterwards my friends had been shocked, and said, "you just recited poetry to Rangers fans, and they paid you money!??!" I'm still not entirely sure what this means, but... I'd like to thank those guys too, though I don't know their names anymore...
(This was back in the early 90's...)

John Carter for his Flaming Road kill recipe.
Eric Wright for his "Gut-less" method of field dressing a deer.

Brian Townsend was the first person to teach me how to make mead. It was a kind fly by night lesson, and I've since made some changes in my methodology, but I would like to thank him for the knowledge he shared with me...

My mom used to churn butter, but I have since learned the mason jar method from a youtube video. I am sorry for not remembering the name of the person's page I learned it from, but thank you just the same.

My Dad used to make Ham and Egg noodles, and it was a staple of my youth. If you think about it, it's high energy, but also high in cholesterol as well. (probably, mostly not the good kind, but it tastes awesome).

Shirley Carter for her Lemon Iced boxed pie recipe. Germ for his Mustard based BBQ sauce.

Ray Carlisle gave me the venison recipe; per my usual I couldn't help, but tamper… His way is simpler.

There are several reference books that I read during the making of this book, one was, "The knowledge: how to rebuild civilization in the aftermath of a cataclysm" By Lewis Dartnell.

"Surviving the Wilds of Florida" by Reid F Tillery.

ABOUT THE AUTHOR:

ERIC MOEBIUS MORLIN
A Florida native.

Moebius ran away at 16
to live in the Little Five Points Community,
in Atlanta, Ga. He stayed there from 1987-2001.

In 2012 he earned a Bachelor of Arts in History
from the University of Central Florida.

He currently resides in New Mexico.

Made in the USA
San Bernardino, CA
24 June 2017